Possibility and Necessity

Volume 1
The Role of Possibility in Cognitive Development

The research reported in this volume was supported by the Fonds National Suisse de la Recherche Scientifique and the Ford Foundation.

Possibility and Necessity

Volume 1
The Role of Possibility in Cognitive Development

Jean Piaget

with
E. Ackermann-Valladao,
I. Berthoud-Papandropoulou,
A. Blanchet, C. Brulhart,
C. Coll, S. Dionnet,
I. Flückiger, M. Flückiger,
A. Henriques-Christophides,
H. Kilcher, D. Leiser,
M. Levy, E. Marbach,
E. Marti, E. Mayer,
L. Miller, C. Monnier,
K. Noschis, E. Rappe-du-
Cher, J. Retschitzki,
G. Tissot, J. Vauclair, and
C. Voelin

Translated from the French
by Helga Feider

University of Minnesota Press • Minneapolis

The University of Minnesota Press gratefully
acknowledges translation assistance provided for this
book by the French Ministry of Culture.

Originally published as *Le possible et le nécessaire, 1:
L'evolution des possibles chez l'enfant*, copyright ©
1981 by Presses Universitaires de France.

Published by the University of Minnesota Press,
2037 University Avenue Southeast, Minneapolis, MN
55414.
Published simultaneously in Canada
by Fitzhenry & Whiteside Limited, Markham.
Printed in the United States of America.

Library of Congress Cataloging-in-Publication Data

Piaget, Jean, 1896–
  Possibility and necessity.
  Translation of: Le possible et le nécessaire.
  Includes bibliographical references and indexes.
  Contents: v. 1. The role of possibility in cognitive
development — v. 2. The role of necessity in
cognitive development.
  1. Possibility—Psychological aspects. 2. Necessity
(Philosophy) 3. Reality—Psychological aspects.
4. Cognition in children. I. Title.
BF723.P67P5413   1987   155.4'13   86–7052
ISBN 0-8166-1370-2 (v. 1)
ISBN 0-8166-1372-9 (v. 2)

Contents

Volume 1
The Role of Possibility in Cognitive Development

	Introduction	3
1.	The Possible Positions of Three Dice on a Surface	8
2.	Possible Pathways of a Vehicle	18
3.	The Possible Forms of Partially Hidden Objects	29
4.	Sectioning a Square	39
5.	Bipartitions and Duplications	54
6.	Free Construction with Hinged Rods	61
7.	Raising Water Levels	70
8.	The Largest Possible Construction from the Same Elements	78
9.	Construction with Sticks and Balls of Modeling Paste	88
10.	A Case of Deductive Possibility	99
11.	Construction of Spatial Arrangements and Equal Distances	108
12.	The Construction of Triangles	123
13.	Construction with a Compass	137
	Conclusions	145
	Index	157

Volume 2
The Role of Necessity in Cognitive Development

Introduction
1. A Problem of Physical Necessity
2. Necessity and Impossibility in Compositions of Rotations
3. The Construction of a Slope
4. Necessities Involved in Length Measures
5. Associativity of Lengths
6. Multiplication and Multiplicative Associativity
7. Distributivity
8. Necessary and Sufficient Conditions in the Construction of Proofs
9. A Proof with Interdependent Information
10. A Case of a Necessary Limit
Conclusions
Index

Possibility and Necessity

Volume 1
The Role of Possibility in Cognitive Development

Introduction

To defend our constructivist epistemology against nativist and empiricist positions, it is not enough to show that new knowledge is always the result of a regulatory process—that is, of equilibration—since it can always be assumed that this regulatory process is itself hereditary (as in the case of organic homeostasis); or, alternatively, that it is the product of learning experiences of varying degrees of complexity. Therefore, we decided to approach the problem of the generation of new knowledge from a different angle, focusing on the development of possibilities. Obviously, any idea or action that gets realized must have existed previously as a possibility, and a possibility, once conceived, will generally breed other possibilities. The problem of the opening up of new possibilities, we believe, is thus of some interest to epistemology.

The fact that possibilities are generated in ever-increasing numbers in the course of human development itself constitutes one of the best arguments against empiricism. Possibilities are in fact not observable, resulting as they do from subjects' active constructions. Even though the properties of objects play a role in these constructions, the properties always get interpreted in the light of a subject's acting on them. Such actions at the same time generate an ever-increasing number of new possibilities with increasingly rich interpretations. We are thus dealing with a creative process very different from the simple reading of reality invoked by empiricism.

If possibilities always precede their realization, one may object, they must necessarily be preformed. Therefore, they cannot be used to justify the constructivist position. Against this, we offer two kinds of arguments, one psychological and the other logical. The first requires that a distinction be made between the observer's and the subject's perspective. If, to the former, the range of possibilities appears very large indeed, it remains to be determined how it appears to the latter. Our observations reveal, in fact, that between the ages of 4 to 5 and 11 to 12 years, there is a progressive enrichment, a qualitative development that

3

is both regular and complex. These observations support the hypothesis that possibilities are gradually built up rather than being preformed.

As for our logical arguments, they are based on the fact that the expression *the set of possibilities* has meaning only with respect to those possibilities that are deducible from a necessary law—for instance, the number of possible surfaces of a cube or sides of a polygon and so on. But when we think of all possible variations that a subject may discover step by step in a situation she tries to analyze, then it makes no sense to speak of a set of possibilities because each variation can generate new possibilities. In general, the *set of all possibles* is even more open, since *all* is in itself another *possible* in motion. There remains another fundamental difficulty: if one accepts the notion of predetermined ideas, and hence of possible hypotheses in any conceivable situation, there remains the problem of the status of errors. On the one hand, they are unpredictable, so that their probability of occurrence cannot be precisely determined. On the other hand, if true ideas are preexisting from eternity, then it must be concluded (as did B. Russell in the Platonic period of his early works) that false ideas also preexist from eternity (that they coexist with true ones like "red roses with white roses"); later, Russell rejected this absurd conclusion, and we can only commend him for it. This is not to deny that a corrected error may turn out to be more productive of future possibilities than immediate success.

In short, *possibility* in cognition means essentially invention and creation, which is why the study of possibility is of prime importance to constructivist epistemology (this is all the more true considering that one can speak of possibilities only relative to a subject, as we shall try to show: the virtual in physics has meaning only in the eyes of the physicist). This point established, our goal was to try to observe the mechanism responsible for the generation of ever new possibilities. To accomplish this, we had to find problems simple enough so that even 4- to 5-year-olds could provide us with an adequate and instructive display of their imaginations and complex enough so that 12-year-olds would perceive an infinity of possible solutions where appropriate. Consequently, we have divided this work into four sections according to the particular techniques used. Chapters 1–3 deal with possibilities derived from spontaneous groupings in subjects' actions or conjectures (arranging objects in various ways, imagining various possible shapes of a partly concealed solid, etc.). Chapters 4–6 deal with possibilities in free combinations, followed by certain constraints (cutouts, etc.). Chapters 7–10 proceed to possibilities with optimalizations (assembling the "largest possible" objects, etc.). Finally, chapters 11–13 treat of possible constructions of geometric shapes.

Before presenting our main hypotheses, let us establish a few terminological conventions. First, we shall distinguish three classes of schemata. First, we call *presentative schemes* (not simply representational, since they may also be sensorimotor schemata) those schemata that involve simultaneous characteristics of objects. Presentative schemes are conserved when combined (as in a hierarchical scheme). They are determined by previous acquisitions but may be applied outside their initial content of acquisition. Second, *procedural schemes* are means applied toward a goal (we may speak of *precursiveness* as opposed to *recursiveness*). They may be ordered in sequence, but those applied earlier are not necessarily conserved later on. Procedures are also context dependent, so that generalization to different contexts is more difficult and clearly distinguishable from the generalization of the presentative schemes. Third, there are the *operational schemes*, which constitute a synthesis of the two previous ones; they are procedural in that they are performed in real time, but the atemporal structure of the combinatorial laws regulating operations has the characteristic of a higher order presentative scheme.

Thus, each individual has at his disposal two main cognitive systems that are complementary to one another. The presentative system, which consists of stable schemes and structures, has the function essentially of understanding the world. The procedural system, which is in constant flux, has the function of assuring proper performance (success), of satisfying needs by inventing or transferring procedures. The first system constitutes the *epistemic* subject and the second refers to the *psychological* subject, since needs are always relative to individual subjects and the insufficiencies they may experience at certain times.* These insufficiencies are different from the state of incompleteness found in structures, when these come to be attended to. However, once a possibility gets actualized through the application of procedural schemes, a new presentative scheme is created, thence the complementarity of the two systems.

But these constructivist considerations are still insufficient for interpreting the process of how possibilities are generated. We must also specify the role of the limitations of which subjects need to liberate themselves. These limitations have to do with an initial lack of differentiation between reality, possibility, and necessity. In fact, any object or substance in a presentative scheme will first appear to subjects not only as what they are, but also as being that way of necessity, excluding the possibility of variation or change. These convictions, *pseudonecessities* or *pseudoimpossibilities*, as we shall call them, are not only specific to children but can be found at all stages in the history of science. The great Aristotle believed in the (pseudo-)necessity of rectilinear and circular motion, thence his erroneous representation of the trajectories of objects in motion ($\rightarrow\updownarrow$), the same as the one proposed by our 4- to 6-year-olds! Geometry has long been thought to be necessarily Euclidean (even as a priori Euclidean, by Kant), algebra up to Hamilton as being necessarily commutative, curves until Bolzano and Weierstrass as necessarily having tangents, and so on. In children,

---

*B. Inhelder is currently conducting a series of studies on procedures and their relations to psychological subjects.

such pseudonecessities go a good deal further: a square turned on one of its corners is no longer a square and its sides appear as unequal to the subject, the moon can only shine at night because that is its preordained role, etc.

To conceive of new possibilities, it is thus not enough to think of procedures oriented toward a particular goal (either optimal or limited to a search of variations): one also needs to compensate for that actual or virtual perturbation that is the resistance of reality to explanation when it is conceived as pseudonecessary. Such a compensatory mechanism, once it has enabled subjects to conquer this obstacle (pseudonecessity) in a particular situation, in addition leads them to realize almost immediately that if one variation is possible, others are also possible, beginning with the most similar or those that are opposite.

It now becomes clear where these hypotheses lead us: if it is true that the notion of the possible derives from having overcome certain resistances of reality to explanation and from filling the gaps that are perceived as a result of having envisioned one variation, which leads immediately to the realization that others are also possible, then it can be concluded that this dual process involves equilibration in its most general form. But although the system of presentative and structural schemes is characterized by intermittent or lasting states of equilibrium, the nature of the possible that is accessed via the procedural system is one of constant mobility, further strengthened by generalizations once a specific result is obtained. What differentiates the possible from the necessary and from the real is thus the fact that it is directly implicated in the process of reequilibration and that it can reveal a subject's potential prior to actual performance. These possibilities, however, are not predetermined but are being developed (constituted) in novel ways each time subjects encounter a resistance or come to perceive gaps in the manner just described (that is, at each positive or negative disturbance).

Within the process of equilibration, these potentialities, which generate procedures and possibilities, are in essence part of the way accommodation functions. Assimilative schemes—that is, presentative ones—tend to accept input, but this provides only one of the possible extensions of their content. On the other hand, on many occasions they need to accommodate to new situations. The potentialities we talked about are in fact the expressions, varying from one level to the next, of the capacity for accommodation: the possible results thus from the accommodative activity seeking actualization, which in turn depends on both the flexibility and the stability of schemes and the degree of resistance offered by reality. Up to now, we had limited our descriptions of this equilibration process to those aspects that are self-regulatory. In the present volume, we add to this an account of the formation of procedures and the availability of new possibilities. These are two complementary aspects of a single model, for two reasons. One is that self-regulations—improving and evaluating a structure—are procedures only and not presentative schemes; they are determined by the possible and its mechanisms. Second, the generation of possibilities remains throughout subordinated to the laws of equilibration, since it is equilibration that brings about reequilibration and leads to new differentiations and their equilibration, which then become integrated into new systems.

This book then proposes to address two main problems. The first is the development of possibilities with age. In terms of functions, we make the following distinctions: (1) the hypothetically possible, where valid solutions are mixed with errors; (2) the realizable, which are selected on the basis of previous results or previously organized presentative schemes; (3) the deducible, which are derived from intrinsic variations; and (4) the postulated possible, where subjects believe that new constructions are possible but cannot yet find the appropriate procedures. In terms of structures, we shall distinguish four stages: (1) possibilities generated locally by a series of analogies; (2) the concrete co-possible, where several possibilities are simultaneously anticipated before being executed; (3) the abstract co-possible, where each possibility realized is seen as just one among many others conceivable; and (4) the possible in its most general form, where the number of possibilities is seen as infinite.

A second aim this book pursues is to clarify the relations between the evolution of procedures or of possibilities and that of operational structures: Is the former development determined by the latter? Many approximately synchronous acquisitions may suggest this determination, as does the fact that generally external variations become intrinsic and capable of being deduced (inferred). Or, on the contrary, is the generation of possibilities and procedures the mechanism necessary for this construction of operational systems? We shall adopt this second hypothesis, which poses the problem of how the early procedures with all their insufficiencies and faulty regulations can develop into logico-mathematical operations with their well-regulated compositions, their logical necessities and closures. That is one of the central questions we are going to discuss.

1

The Possible Positions
of Three Dice on a Surface

with C. Monnier and S. Dionnet

One of the simplest problems one can pose to get subjects to generate multiple procedures is certainly to ask them about possible changes in the position of a small number of objects on a restricted surface. Therefore we chose three dice (with two, only linear configurations would be possible, and we did not ask about possible paths as in chapter 2). We did, however, use three different surfaces: a square measuring 28 cm², a circle with a 28-cm diameter, and an isosceles triangle with a base and a height of 28 cm. This was done to see if the same arrangement would be maintained on surfaces varying in shape. In addition, a secondary factor was introduced, which the subjects might ignore or take into consideration as they wished. This secondary factor was color, each of the surfaces of the dice having a different color and the supporting areas being colored as well: the first one red, the second green, and the third blue. In fact, this addition turned out to be useful in that some of our younger subjects adopted different procedures depending on whether they made reference to color or to shape.

A tricky problem was to decide upon an appropriate vocabulary to be used in the instructions addressed to the subjects. Since any of the positions of the three dice determined some kind of a shape, no matter how irregular, we began by asking subjects to "arrange the dice in as many ways as possible on the cardboard." However, it turned out that even older subjects reacted to this instruction by producing only regular patterns, in spite of the neutral tenor of our demands for change ("Could you do it another way?"). This suggested to us that perhaps the expression "arrange" was interpreted as "arrange orderly." Therefore we changed the instruction to say: "Put these dice on the cardboard in every possible way." This, however, did not change the relatively late emergence of scattered configurations. Even the instruction "Put them any way at all" is not interpreted as an incitation to produce irregular shapes at all age levels.

Once subjects had exhausted their possibilities, we proceeded to ask for value judgments: "Which are the best ways to arrange the dice, the most correct, the most interesting, the most difficult" and so forth. This could yield interesting information about subjects' goals inherent in their procedures, the final instruction being to find the "best" or the "worst" of the patterns.

Level I

As in other studies, we found that the children begin to see new possibilities as a result of applying analogical procedures combining small variations with similarities. This kind of behavior is particularly enhanced in the present study, since new configurations can be created by changing the position of a single die (whereas changing a path from A to B requires a complete reorganization of elements).

Mar (4;11): "Place them . . . ," etc. He puts the three dice at each of three corners of the square. "And another way?" He moves one die from the lower right to the unoccupied upper right. "And another way . . . ?" He permutes the dice on the diagonal. Then he shifts the die from the upper left to the lower right, and then moves the die from the upper right to the upper left corner. Then, at last an innovation: he places one of the dice in the center of the square, commenting upon this discovery by saying *This looks like a heart.* "How was it before?" *Like that* (he only remembers what he did first, but not the pattern he had just modified). "How many ways could one do it—10, 100, 1,000?" *Three.* "How many have you done?" . . . "Would there be still other ways?" *No*. But he still comes up with a new pattern: the three dice all lined up next to one another. "Good. Do another one just a bit different from that one." He moves the rightmost die 1 cm to the right. "Now, can you do one that is very different?" He squeezes them along the lower and adjacent lateral border. We proceed to the triangle. Mar declares that he cannot put the dice into the corner *because it is pointed; it only works on the square* (he points to its right angles). He still manages to find a pattern along the median, then another one in the form of a triangle, then along one of the edges. When asked to do a "wrong one," he aligns two dice, placing the third one at a 45-degree angle. "Why is that wrong?" *I guessed the wrong one in my head. That one* [the three in a row] *is right*. He also designates as wrong two further irregular patterns. Inside the circle, likewise, the right positions are those on the diameter or along the perimeter, and the wrong ones are those with one die *separated from the others*.

Eri (5;1): When given the same instruction to "arrange the dice in all possible ways," but beginning with the circle, he produces 15 patterns—all, however, of linear or triangular shape. The linear ones are either closely aligned or spread out. Two patterns only reach the border of the circle, and none follows its perimeter. On the square, Eri gives eight variations, in seven of which the dice touch one or the other of the sides. These remain, however, rather similar in shape to the ones produced on the circle (triangular shapes). None of the patterns is linear or includes three of the four corners. Yet Eri claims that he *has made more patterns on the square, because it is much bigger.* On the triangle he is told several times to place the dice in any way he likes. He only finds six shapes, triangular ones — including some with one corner only — and one linear, horizontal one at the center of the cardboard. Asked if he could find one that is "wrong," he offers a triangular pattern that is hardly different from one of his earlier ones and just slightly less regular. Upon the suggestion to place the dice in each of the three corners of the triangle, he agrees that this would be placing them "any which way." When asked to give consideration to the colors on the square, he first produces only rightly spaced alignments of identical color; when asked to do a "really bad one," he builds an oblique one with spaces in between. "Why is this bad?" *Because it is not the same color.*

Nat (5;4) produces about the same patterns on the square as Eri did (no pattern including three corners), but does not think it possible to redo them on the circle. We propose two dice closely aligned at an angle with the third facing (the three aligned on the diagonal), and she says that this is impossible on the round surface: "Try to do something like it." She arranges the dice along the diameter at 45 degrees. "Is that the same?" *It's not the same, because it is round.* Similarly, a curved shape we suggested to her on the square seems to her impossible to reproduce on the triangular base *because this is a triangle and that is a square.* For this subject, then, the figure could not be dissociated from the ground. To these regular cases of 4 and 5 year olds, we have to add that of a subject whose method differs radically depending on the instruction "all possible ways" or "the best possible."

Yve (4;6): "I would like you to place them in all possible ways." He rolls the dice on the square base. "And another way?" He rolls them again. "Is it right like that?" *Yes, because you're not allowed to do the same ones again.* He repeats this procedure seven times, saying, *Now, there is a yellow one,* etc. "How about that?" (We arrange three yellow sides up in a row.) *That's cheating, because they're all three together.* We arrange them in a triangle. *That's cheating, because it's the same color.* What can we do to do them right? *You have to roll the dice.* But as soon as we ask him to do the "best possible," he no longer minds the colors nor does he roll the dice any more; he places them on the square in an oblique, linear array or in a triangular pattern (or even in piles), and without any regard to the corners or the sides of the base. This is all the more striking as he begins by denying the possibility that the same patterns can be produced on the triangular base (he later corrects himself, but only after several trials).

The 6-year-old subjects find a richer set of variations, notably nonlinear contiguities (⊞, ⊟, ⊞, etc.), but they still proceed only by successive analogies without anticipation of co-possible patterns.* Similarly, they still consider

---

Translator's note: The term *co-possible* is a neologism introduced by the authors to express the child's capacity to envision a variety of possibilities simultaneously, in contrast to the younger subjects' limited productions created in sequential fashion.

the regular shapes as the best ones and the less regular ones as "bad," without showing any understanding (as the subjects of level II begin to do) that from the point of view of "all possible ways" all patterns are equivalent. Third, subjects still do not think it possible to reproduce the same shapes on the three types of base: "No," said 6-year-old Xav, "you cannot make a triangle on a square, and on a circle you can do more, you can follow it all around," whereas for Har, who is also 6 years old, "the square is harder, because it has a lot of space and it's hard to know where to put them." He envisions a horizontal row of three dice on the square but "not on the circle, because it is not a square" (they are both 28 cm in diameter and length respectively). As for Ben, also 6 years old, we copy the closely spaced linear array he produced on the triangular base onto the square base, but he objects: "No, it's not the same thing."

In sum, the first level observed in subjects between 4 and 6 years, including Yve's conduct with respect to colors, has a general characteristic of constructing possibilities by analogy, using stepwise progressions from one construction to the next. At no time do subjects aspire to find a pattern that is the most different, nor do they realize that the unoccupied space constitutes a field for possible, infinitely variable positions. This idea does not make its appearance until children have reached level III. There remains the case of Yve, who seems to have an understanding of the infinite number of possibilities, when he rolls the dice at random, even though in the second part of the interview, which concerns shape, he affirms (as do the other subjects) that the shape of the base limits the possible configurations; that is, he perceives a mutual dependence between figure and ground. Thus, the apparently probabilistic conduct of Yve rolling the dice to mix the colors (*or else it's cheating*) can easily be explained by his sensing the difficulty of predicting the possible combinations of six different colors on three dice and therefore preferring simply to roll the dice to avoid the effort: by not taking into account the combinations and simply naming their colors without regard to their positions, he simplifies the problem and thus remains far from those subjects who come to realize that all patterns and shapes are equally good.*

Level II

Between 7 and 10 years of age, one observes a series of new acquisitions that logically belong together but that do not always manifest themselves at the same time in any given subject. This means that the limitations characteristic of level I continue to be present in certain respects, whereas they are already overcome in others. This process varies from one subject to another. In general, these acquisitions consist in progressing from analogical and successive to anticipated and simultaneous projections of possibilities. They include dissociating the pos-

*Of course, the possibility that this subject was rather advanced for his age and may belong at level II cannot be entirely discarded.

sible patterns from the shape of the base. We also see a systematic search for maximal differentiation of patterns and the acceptance of the irregular as possible and equivalent as much as the "good" ones.

Ser (6;11), when asked to "place them in all possible ways," rolls the dice three times onto the square, producing successively three triangular patterns concentrated near the center, no doubt since his hand remained in the vicinity of that area. "Are there many ways to do it?" *No, not many.* He rolls once again. "Every time it's different?" *Yes.* "Are there about 10, 100, 1,000, or a million ways?" *Ten.* "Can you do them all?" *No.* "How many can you do?" *Three.* "Which is the best way?" He rolls them gently. The same behaviors were observed on the triangle. "What did I ask you to do?" *All possible ways, no matter what colors* (it can be seen that he focuses on shape). "Place them any way you can." He does a small triangle. "Now, do them again but any which way." The result is barely different. "Can you tell when it is any which way and when it is not?" *No, it's impossible to tell* [!]. "Now do one that's very different from that one." This time he pushes them with his hand over the cardboard and offers five different agglutinated patterns. "Is there a way that can only be done on that one [the triangle]?" *Yes.* He rolls the dice. "There are several ways?" *It's the same on all three* [bases]. To conclude: "Why did you roll the dice?" *To do different ways.* "By rolling and by pushing them you can place them the same way?" *Yes, it's the same.*

Cri (6;7) comes up with a method that opens the way toward the concept of co-possibilities: she rolls the dice, first two, then one at a time, always in the same place. She thus creates 17 different patterns on the circle (the last two by moving the dice around). Then she estimates the number of patterns as 10. After some hesitation, she admits that one could do the same thing on the square. As for the triangle, she first affirms the belief that it is different in that one can put a die in each corner. She reconsiders this and concludes that *it is all the same.*

Alb (7 years) gives two interesting reactions. One is when he passes from symmetric, regular patterns to an irregular one (two dice aligned and the third one touching the second one at one corner only), commenting: *This one is better, I like it because it's* [more] *different.* The second reaction is when he is asked to make a pattern that is "not right and that you haven't made yet," and he replies: *That means it is right, if it hasn't been made yet.* Then he invents a superposition, saying: *It's correct because this die does not touch the two sides* [of the others] *as before.* But he believes that some patterns are impossible to do on the circle *because it doesn't have corners.*

Nic (7 years) immediately sees seven possibilities on the triangle as a function of the angles, the sides, and the area within the triangle, where he sees the possibility of making small triangular patterns. He foresees 100 possibilities, of which he believes he is able to realize *10 or so.* This is a first indication of abstract co-possibility. He announces that he can do the same on the circular base, but he ends up building around 20 patterns by moving one or two of the dice one after the other, without any overall plan. Each new pattern differs from the preceding one in some systematic way. (These variations are not random, or at least not completely so.) On the square he thinks he can do more *because there are four corners, but not on the circle.* But after having made a small triangle in one of the corners he adds: *Oh, no, it works also on the other one* [the circle]. Likewise a curved pattern, which he first believes specific to the circle, is then reproduced on the square. To obtain different configurations, Nic states that one has to move at least one die each time. When asked not to touch the die, he answers *So, by blowing.*

Jac (7;9) believes it is possible to make about the same number of patterns (between 100 and 200) on all three bases. He agrees also to do them "any which way," by rolling them. Like Nic, he considers wrong only placements *outside of the borders*; he varies the colors but thinks that position is more important, *but the color is important, too.*

Phi (7;6) provides a nice illustration of a transition to deductive thinking with respect to colors. After a few random alignments such as *AAA*, *BCD*, *EEB*, and *DFE** (without any plan), he announces 10 possibilities. When asked: "How many ways?", he explains: *You do the three yellow ones, then two yellow and one other color, then one yellow and two other colors. After that you continue like that with another color.* "Is there still another way?" *No.* "Sure?" *Yes.* When given the triangle, he immediately finds seven linear or triangular patterns. He tries hard to reproduce the same patterns on the square, *because you can say that the square consists of two triangles pasted together* (he points out the diagonal). On the circle, the same procedure could be repeated: *On the three* [bases] *it's the same.* "How many ways?" *Ten.* "Not 100?" *No, there are 10; if you want to do 100, you have to repeat the same ones.*

Ter (7;8) thinks differently: if there are about 10 ways (of which she first produces only 4), *you can do 10 on each one* [of the three bases], *but they are not the same ones.* In all, *about 20.*

Ris (8;0), unlike Ter, who distinguishes the "good" patterns from the "bad" ones by their regularity, says that a pattern is better *because it's almost completely changed: here it's like a triangle and there it's a line.* And later: *That's better* [five combinations] *because they are almost all different.*

Ste (8;3) similarly: *That's better, because it's not simple*; for the "worst" he produces only *a pattern that's turned around*, forgetting that he had used such symmetries also when producing "good" patterns.

Man (8;6) prefers tight patterns and when asked to do "wrong" ones produces

---

Translator's note: The letters refer to the six colors of the dice.

scattered configurations, but not random ones—rather, with the dice spaced widely apart.

Ver (8;11) responds similarly but discovers that to make "good" patterns, one does not need the cardboards, which constitutes a liberation from a constraint.

Lau (8;3), when asked to arrange the dice "any way you can," first claims that he'd already done so; then he discovers that *they can be all mixed up* and that in this way one can do *many, about 200*, whereas he had produced about 20 or 25. "Would there be more or less than 200?" *More.* "One thousand would be too many?" *Perhaps.* "And a million?" *That would be way too many.*

Tie (8;9) comes to see the equivalence of all co-possible arrangements, after a series of tries that are *all different.* "Are some of them better than others?" *They are all the same.* "Show me other possibilities." He adds a few. "Is one better than the others?" *No, they're all the same.* Yet, the idea of disorder does not occur to him.

Isa (9;2), like Tie, thinks that all patterns are equally good. "It's not possible to do an even better one?" *No, I don't think so.* "And a very bad one?" *I can't.* "Why?" *Because you can only do right ones.* Estimates around 1,000 possibilities.

Fre (10;5) responds similarly. The scattered pattern is not wrong and the only wrong positions are *outside of the base.* "When they are on the base, they are all correct?" *Yes.* But *there cannot be more than 100.*

We have cited many examples in order to show the following facts: first, the generality of the progress made at this level of development—inferred co-possibilities come to replace the earlier analogical, sequential mode; and second, the variability of responses, which do not necessarily belong to one level. We expected to find a more stringent internal logic. In the other studies presented here, we usually distinguish a sublevel IIA of "concrete" co-possibilities, limited in number but all realized, as well as a sublevel IIB of "abstract" co-possibilities, far more numerous (but not infinite), of which the subject realizes only a few examples. Even though in the present study we find, by and large, a similar development, we were not able to group our subjects exhaustively according to the two sublevels because subjects tended to give evidence of mixed response patterns. For example, Ser (the youngest of this group) begins by rolling the dice, which seems like an advanced type of procedure. He also responds appropriately when asked about different patterns, understands the independence of patterns from the shape of the bases, as well as the general notion of "any which way." Yet, despite these successes, he only predicts 10 co-possibilities, only 3 of which he believes he is able to realize! This modesty places him somewhere halfway between the concrete and abstract concepts of possibility. On the other hand, Nic at 7 years (who realizes 10 out of an estimated 100 possibilities) and certainly Isa or Fre (with 100 out of 1,000) have already reached the level of abstract concepts of possibility.

However, the notion of co-possibilities too numerous for all to be realized seems to imply equivalence of all configurations as all being "possibles" (while also being different), and hence to entail acceptance of irregular and "scattered" patterns. The pseudonecessities of gestaltlike patterns ought to have been overcome, since the "bad" patterns are just as possible. Yet, few subjects at this level go that far; moreover no clear relationship to age seems to exist. Most of these subjects only affirm that the "best" patterns are the ones that are "most different" (which is already a definite progress with respect to the preceding level I). Thus, Ser makes explicit this search for whatever is different; Alb and Ris say, "It's better because it's different"; and Ste says, "because it's not simple." But, in fact, they continue to adhere to the regular patterns, and Man, even at 8 years, finds the "scattered" ones "false." This goes against the logical consequence of co-possibilities, which is that all patterns are equally "good" regardless of regularity. The developmental progression we observe is one of an implicit notion such as is evident in Ser's conduct (it is impossible to distinguish between the "any which way" evident in his rolling the dice and his explicit negation of such knowledge); then in Alb (his arguments concerning "the right way"); followed by the full realization that all patterns are "equally good," as observed in Tie ("They are all the same, none better than the others"), who makes no reference to irregularity, however. Finally, Lau, Isa, and Fre explicitly accept irregular patterns as being correct.

These problems of inconsistent structuring of the notion of co-possibilities indicate that such conducts certainly result from some form of deductive schema replacing the earlier analogical one; however, they are as yet only local and sporadic, and no evidence is found of the kind of synthesis between possibility and necessity that characterizes the onset of operational structures. The best deductive inferences observed in our subjects are the semicombinatorial ones of Cri and Phi. However, extensionally, they are very limited. For example, Cri, after having built 17 patterns, estimates the total number of patterns as being 10. Phi gives a nice demonstration of deductive reasoning when he proceeds to apply to the square base the patterns he found possible on the triangle, since the diagonal divides the square into two triangles. Still, he only considers 10 co-possibilities because if there were hundreds they would simply be repetitions of the 10 distinct possibilities!

The problem of the transfer of possibilities from one of the bases to the other two is of interest in relation to the distinction made earlier between procedural transfers and presentative generalizations. Both produce new possibilities; but whereas the former proceed independently of any consideration of necessities, the latter are strictly coordinated with perceptions of necessities. Procedural schemes are in fact highly context dependent and are difficult to detach from their first context and to apply to new ones. In the present case, this context is defined in terms of the relation of figure to ground. We have observed how sub-

jects fail or hesitate to transfer even up to the age of 10; 5 in the case of Fre
("The round one doesn't have four corners: there are more possibilities on the
square"), whereas already some 6- to 7-year-olds come to see the equivalence
(for Ser and Cri, "It's the same thing on all three").

In sum, we have shown two principal characteristics for this level: the deductive nature of co-possibilities and the lack of consistency with respect to their
logical consequences, without mentioning the limited number of co-possibilities
envisioned. From this we are inclined to conclude that these limited progressions
in the development of possibility cannot be the direct result of the formation of
concrete operations. Rather, they may constitute a necessary framework for this
development (inasmuch as operations also are procedures, which are applied to
possible transformations). Within this framework, operations may be elaborated
by joining certain forms of necessity to the notion of possibility. Operations then
act in return upon the perception of new openings and new possibilities, as we
shall see with the next level (III).

Level III

Among the 11- to 12-year-old subjects, a significant portion remains at the level
II type of functioning with its various characteristics, such as the limited number
of possibilities envisioned. But among these latecomers, we find certain remarks
that announce level III.

Ena (11;2) only sees about *10 or 50* possibilities but notes, in moving one
of the dice by only a few millimeters in a triangular pattern, *that makes a little
difference*. But she adds that *it's still the same shape, so it's not another way*.
We can see here an implicit understanding of a multiplicity of possible small variations, which should lead to the notion of infinity; but a conflict arises because
of the existence of a limited number of categories (linear patterns, triangular
ones, etc.).

Ita (12;8) affirms categorically that *there is no false way* even if the dice are
scattered all over, and so forth. But it is impossible to arrange them in "all possible ways," which amounts to negating the possibility of realizing all the possibilities but not their abstract potentiality. There remains thus a certain fixation at
level II, but with a tendency toward level III.

The following subjects, on the other hand, succeed in conceptualizing an infinity of possibilities—either in intension ("any way whatsoever") or in extension
(infinite number).

Cia (13;11) first makes a few patterns and then rolls the dice, saying, *That
way you can say it's any which way*; from this, Cia concludes that *if you look
at all the centimeters, it becomes almost infinite*. We have here the continuation
of Ena's reasoning about the "little differences." But Cia arrives at the idea of
"whatsoever" yet remains conservative with respect to numerical evaluation.

Cat (11;6) starts out by rolling the dice any which way, saying: *As long as they stay on the base, it's correct; if they fall outside, then it's false.* He concludes that *changing the place of each die, or by rolling them randomly, it is infinite.* Here we see made explict both the notion of "any way whatsoever" and of infinity in extension.

Guy (12;0) makes a few fairly regular patterns, then without resorting to rolling the dice concludes that by moving each die slightly *by centimeters, it's infinite: you can change a color or a millimeter, you would have to note all that, that would take months.* "Is it possible to do that?" *With these sizes, that would require sophisticated calculations.* "What if the base were quite small?" *It would be the same: if you count around the dice, the distances would be relatively greater. But it would be the same, I would proceed by millimeters instead of centimeters: it's like on the violin* (where intervals change along each string). "What about height?" *That would make any pattern whatever.*

It is easy to see the difference between this level and the preceding one. At level IIB, children understand that the patterns they make are only a sample of all possible patterns, of which there are too many to do them all. But they believe that all could be realized on the model of the patterns effectively built. Hence, the relatively modest number envisioned. What is new at level II is that children do not simply deduce from the few patterns they have made the possibility of varying them still more, according to the same model; rather, by using abstract reflection, they infer a law of construction by minimal but iterative variations. These consist of "looking at all the centimeters" (Cia), "changing a millimeter" (Guy), or simply repeating the rolling of the dice (Cat). In this case, the possibilities can no longer be materially realized, which annoys Ita, but they can be conceptualized in a way analogous to the set of natural numbers, which are generated by the rule $n + 1$. Essentially this means that possibilities come to be related to a notion of necessity—the two concepts undergo a synthesis—or the notion of increasing probabilities comes to join that of possibility (as in Cat's case, who perceives the outcomes of rolling the dice as similar to small "changes in position"). This is what explains the transition from the conception of a small number of possibilities with their still extrinsic variations characteristic of level IIB to the deductive infinity of intrinsic variations that is proper to the constructions of level III.

2

Possible Pathways of a Vehicle

with C. Monnier and J. Vauclair

Among the possibilities accessible to a child, the variety of ways to get from point *A* to point *B* is obviously one that is already acquired in such sensorimotor skills as walking. We decided to see whether, in a domain of actions as elementary as this, one can find (as one does in more complex domains) a developing mechanism generating novel possibilities, starting from those possibilities that are initially realized or anticipated. We examined two questions in this regard: first, do children see at once a variety of co-possibilities, or do they first proceed by successive innovations? Second, do these co-possibilities lead rapidly to indefinite extension, or do they first appear to be limited in number?

To facilitate this analysis, we decided not to represent the limits *A* and *B* by simple points in space and the paths by simple gestures or drawings, since this would have presupposed the existence of an abstract notion of space as containing, in general, the material objects surrounded by it. In reality, however, only objects exist with their relative positions, their distances, and (in the case of moving objects) their directions (in general, toward a goal). Thus, before Descartes and Fermat introduced the coordinate system, geometry only studied the forms of objects, not space as such. Thus, we chose as a moving object a small, toy car; as limits *A* and *B* some toy objects (trees, etc.); and as space a room with furniture, where a post *P* could be placed as an obstacle between *A* and *B*. This setup makes it possible to observe certain limitations of interest: preoperational subjects construct paths determined by the objects, whereas subjects at the formal level, as usual, come to see an infinity of ways. A good example is our 12-year-old subject Pop, who, in response to our demand to find a way to get from *A* to *B*, instead of starting out with a straight line, asserts immediately: *It's infinite*.

In the first part of the study, children are told simply to point to the path. The toy car, which is radio operated, serves only to represent a moving object. In the second part of the experimental session, children are asked to make the car move (a button to be pushed or pulled makes the car move forward and back up, respectively, and a steering wheel moves it to the right or left). This procedure creates new problems of possibility, problems relative to the succession of trials and experimental observations (see below – The Car Mechanism).

Level IA

The subjects at level IA proceed by successive variations, their only principle being to vary the goal objects or to introduce small changes.

Pie (4;11): "Show me all the ways one can go from A to B." *Straight ahead.* "Can you make another?" *No.* "Try it." *You could put the car in the garage* (he repeats the straight path). "But do another one." He describes a slightly curved line. "And another." *No.* "There are only two to do?" *Yes.* "Why?" *Because there's only one car.* We set up the post. "Now, do it." *It's impossible, because there's a post, so we can't go to* B, *it would make an accident.* "Try." He makes a curved path. *I got around it.* "And another." He repeats the same curved path, but turns back at the post, having bypassed it, instead of going to B. "Another." A curve from A to B, by passing the post at the right instead of left. *That's not the same.* "Are there others?" *No.* "When you go to school, you always take the same way?" *No.* "And from A to B? Always the same?" *Yes.*

Mar (4;6): *Straight ahead.* "Another one?" *Straight ahead and it turns* (a slight curve toward B). "And still another?" A symmetric replica of the first curve. "Another?" A curved line halfway around B. "Are there many?" *Six if I want.* "Maybe 20?" *No.* "Try another?" He repeats his second line without remembering it. "How do you go about finding them?" *I think about the roads where we go in the car.* "Do another." A big curve from A to B. "And another." He makes the curve wider. "Another." *I've done them all.* "You could move things around to find new paths?" *Yes.* He moves B back a bit. "You could make more new paths?" *Yes.* "Which ones?" *I can't remember.* "Just do one." *Straight ahead.* "You did that one before." *No, before it was there, now it's here, so I can do another straight ahead.* "Is that a different path?" *Yes.* "There are how many paths one can do if A is farther away?" *Another six.* "But before it was seven." *Oh, then it's seven.* "Are there more or fewer of the same as before?" *Fewer.* "Why?" *There's less space.* He points to the area he considers free if B is moved farther away. We set up the post P. *He has to turn.* "It couldn't be done before?" *No* (he had done the same curve before), *I didn't do it before, because the post wasn't there.* "One could do a lot of paths with the post?" *Three.* "Why?" *Because there isn't much room there* [between A and P] *and there* [between P and B].

Pat (5;5) goes from A to B with a slight turn to end up behind B. "Another." She goes from A to the wall and from there to B. "Another?" She repeats the same path. "Another?" She goes from A to the door and from there to B. *Here.*

She goes on to vary the paths by passing by a corner of the room or near a bench, a table, a basket, etc. We move B to a location B': she starts over again as she did with AB. We place B below: she produces a path of the same shape and says that it is the same as before without taking note of the vertical direction.

Col (4;11) bypasses a table before heading toward B, then a few other pieces of furniture and finally two tables at once. "Is that the shortest one?" *No, one can go under this table.* "And if one is nearly out of gas?" *Like that* [straight]. Reviewing his moves, he points to the four corners of the room to indicate that he has gone everywhere.

The interesting point about these possibilities is that rather than representing paths in space they are simply routes toward one or more goals or ways of avoiding an obstacle. The objects are so important that the subject cannot imagine doing the same path in their absence (Mar, with the post added, does not recognize the path he had just performed without it). The only references to space as such seem to be those of Col, to the room, but he only does so to say that he has contacted all the objects in it; the other is that of Mar, who (referring to his outings in the family car) thinks that paths vary with their length but in ways that are anything but consistent: now, a long distance contains fewer paths because it is narrow, and a bit later it is the opposite, because the short distances (AP and PB) have less "room" the other way.

In sum, at this level spatial possibilities are reduced to going from one object to another, these being approached more or less directly or bypassed by curves that are more or less pronounced. The only other variation consists in a greater or lesser number of possible paths envisioned. The subjects experience great difficulties remembering the form of a path already produced, but they easily remember the different goal objects. This fact teaches us two things. The first is that the variations in the form of the pathways, as opposed to the goal objects, are given very little attention by the subjects at this level. The second is the essentially successive nature of the possibilities envisioned, which is not surprising; but we already see certain predictions and even (after the fact) a capacity to group possibilities into families of co-possibilities. These initial limitations are of interest in that they point to the way the regulatory processes with their negative and positive feedback will take to bring about systematic and ultimately operational procedures and deductive reasoning about possibilities.

Levels 1B and II

The subjects of level 1B proceed, like those of level IA, by a successive strategy, generating one possibility after another. But instead of simply changing goal objects, they attend to the form of the paths, producing a variety of possibilities.

Nic (4;10) begins by a path *straight ahead*, then goes on to trace a straight line halfway, then a short perpendicular one, which turns into an oblique line toward B. The next trial begins in the same way, followed by three segments that form a trapeze, commented on as follows: *That's not exactly the same*. The following path is composed of five straight segments, the first and the last horizontal, the second and the fourth equal in length and perpendicular to the former, while the third segment links their upper ends, like this: ⌐⌐⌐ . The next path doubles this square-shaped detour as a symmetrical path below the main line. Then he adds angles similar to two steps of a stairway. From there, Nic proceeds to show four irregular steps leading directly to B. These steps suggest to him the idea of making wavy lines, of which he indicates five or six, extending one of his first straight segments. When we move B to B', the sinusoidal lines outnumber the others. When we add the post, Nic believes that does not change anything, which is not surprising after all the detours he has produced and which he estimates as *100*.

Ave (4;6) proceeds the same way: having shown a straight line AB, he adds two fairly large U-shaped detours, one next to the other. He next makes them smaller and farther apart. The fourth starts with W's and continues straight. The fifth is a big curve. The sixth one adds a loop, and the seventh one subdivides that in two, one after the other, and so on. When we move A to A', he invents a new path, ⌐ . With the post he returns to the straight line AB with a small detour around P, but that (post) is *not important*.

Rel (5;2) only does curved lines, but with many variations: (1) a large curve making a wide circle around B and leading back to A; (2) a similar curve but with a loop; (3) a figure ◯◯, horizontally; (4) a variation of this with a loop at the crossing; (5) a curve symmetrical to (1) around A.

The mode of generating successive possibilities characteristic of level IB is thus the same as at level IA: one path A leads to another B, after the fact, by means of an analogy, which preserves some characteristic x while introducing a modification x'; after which this new path B generates another path C by means of another analogy. Each new analogy consists of similarities and differences, where the similarities may be relative to x or x' or again to y, a characteristic not yet considered. The differences then appear as x'' or y'', and so forth, proceeding from C to D, etc. There is thus no evidence of any kind of program nor of recursive procedures, only analogical transfers with perpetual successive variations as to what is retained as similar or introduced as innovation. There is, however, progress with respect to level IA in that paths are now analyzed as such in terms of their spatial transformations instead of being considered only in relation to objects to be reached or avoided as in level IA (where, it is true, some variations could already be observed that concerned the form of paths only).

Further development consists not so much in the discovery of new paths (these remain essentially the same for all of the following levels), but rather in new modes of generation and procedural transfers. That is, while the generation of new possibilities is successive at level I without any preplanning of co-possibilities, the progress that characterizes level II—progress that is slow and laborious—is the developing capacity to constitute such co-possibilities. The subject conceptualizes from the start or in the course of the interview a set of variations before attempting to carry them out. We are dealing here with a progress in the inferential mechanism, which, beginning with analogical procedures, gradually leads to deductive generation of possibilities and finally, around 11–12 years of age (that is, quite a bit later), to the notion of arbitrary variations that are infinite in number. However, this progress in conceptual development regarding possibility is not accompanied by an enrichment in content; that is, a subject who can predict a "family" of possibilities may not envision others and may thus produce fewer pathways than the level I child.

Cri (7;1) says immediately: *The easiest way to go is straight ahead, otherwise you can go zigzag* [she shows in fact the curved paths] . . . *and still perhaps some other*. This time she shows zigzags made of straight-line segments. Then she recapitulates: *One was straight ahead, the other round, and that one has corners.* "Are there others?" *I have an idea, but it doesn't work:* ⟨⟨⟨ , etc. When we move *A* and *B* into oblique positions, she decides that would be *the same things* [the same paths].

Rin (8;5) declares: *Straight, then like that* [S horizontal], *in zigzags, two zigzags, and then straight, three zigzags and then straight again*. While carrying out her ideas she finds other variations, this time in succession, as did the subjects of level IB. When *A* and *B* are displaced, Rin hesitates between thinking that the paths are the same or different, then discovers that the differences are in direction only *because the path here goes down*. But she believes by adding more posts one reduces the number of possible paths.

Ric (9;5) enumerates co-possibilities *straight, turn, then the other way* [his symmetric paths] . . . *and do zigzags*; he estimates *about 100*. After a curve, *one could make many others like that*. Thus he comes to agree to 1,000 possibilities *because the room is big*. With the posts he first hesitates but then comes to see that with or without the posts he can make the same detours: *Ah, yes! I can do them*.

Iba (10;4) thinks spontaneously of extreme cases: *Straight, or drive all around the classroom*. He also thinks of intermediate solutions. However, paths resulting from simple variations in the distance from *A* to *B would be longer, but they would be the same*. In fact, he stays with the straight paths except for a family of co-possible curves. He increases his estimate from 50 to 100 as he produces more examples.

What is interesting about these observations is the nature of the progress they mark in the formation of possibilities. This progress concerns mainly the intensive aspect (simultaneous conceptualization of several qualitative variations, all equally possible) rather than the extensive (the number of co-possibilities). The reason is that the first conceptions of co-possibilities (those of Cri and of Rin, which one might class at level IIA) are of a concrete nature in the sense that only those possibilities the subject gets ready to realize are invoked in his descriptions. Intermediate cases are not envisioned, at least not explicitly. In this case the number of possibilities is, of course, severely reduced. On the other hand, with the responses such as given by Ric and Iba, the concrete notion of co-possibilities is soon followed by a procedure that is at once extensional and intensional in the sense that these subjects reason on an abstract level that any one qualitative change is only one among many others (we might thus classify these subjects as belonging to a level IIB). These procedures involve introducing slight variations, either on a continuum or by inserting intermediate values between two adjacent path descriptions. This then leads to considerable increases in the numerical values of estimated co-possibilities, from 100 to 1,000 in Ric's case and from 50 to 100 in the case of Iba (where the numbers are only of symbolic value).

If the transition from level IB to IIA already marks a certain progress in the direction of deductive reasoning by means of analogical procedures, that from level IIA to IIB is still more important since it leads to new types of co-possibilities that go beyond the limits of detailed, immediate, actualized realization. Still, one limitation needs to be pointed out in the accomplishments of level IIB: the abstract notion of co-possibilities attained by the 9- to 10-year-olds (even though not by all) remains restricted to a particular class of possibilities (usually a class of curved paths, but in one 11-year-old subject we noted a class of straight parallels that could be multiplied); it does not yet get generalized to include all possible sets of possibilities. In certain cases, we observed behaviors that were clearly residues of lower developmental levels. Lau at 10;5 years says, for instance, that with two posts set up between A and B it is possible to "make a slalom," but that "if there were only one post, that wouldn't be possible," and he even goes so far as to affirm that a path around the post would not be possible; that is, the same path could not be taken if the post was not there "because you can't make contact with an object that's not there[!]." In general, strategies focusing on the spatial configuration of the pathways are more likely to generate multiple and abstract co-possibilities; those focusing on the goal objects tend to produce the more limited and concrete solutions of lower levels. These observations show that the evolution toward a concept of generalized co-possibilities is a slow and difficult process.

Level III

The evolution to level III comes to term at 11–12 years, an evolution that, as we just pointed out, is not achieved in a single, discontinuous leap, but comes about as a result of a long, laborious developmental process during level IIB.

Gil (10;10) starts out as do those at level II: *One can go straight or make some little detours, passing from behind.* He produces five examples with successively wider detours around *B*, *A*, and both. "How many paths are possible?" *Hundreds. Here already there are about 100 around* B. *It's infinite because you can do as many turns as you like.* "What if we move *A* and *B*?" *I think that would be about the same thing.* Putting up the post *takes one path away* [the straight line], *but it adds some others. But it can turn even without the post . . . so, that doesn't take anything away nor does it add anything.*

Pop (12;0): "Show me all possible paths [from *A* to *B*]." *It's infinite*[!]. "For example?" *Straight, zigzag, S-turns, half circles on each side, any kind of S of different length.* "How do you get these ideas?" *First, the fastest way and then more and more complex.*

The new concept is here what our subjects call "infinite." This notion includes both that of indeterminate in intension and that of unlimited in extension. It is easy to see how this notion derives from that of abstract co-possibilities, as elaborated at level IIB. In fact, *abstract* means that for subjects the few realizations they produce are only examples of a whole set of possible variations (e.g., 1,000 for Ric), which can be inferred in their entirety but cannot be produced, nor even imagined, one by one. It seems quite natural that sooner or later the question about how all these variations can be generated gets reformulated. From the global search for results ("One could do many more of those," as Ric at level II remarked), we find here a more analytic orientation toward change itself that leads from one variation to the next—that is, toward a mode of production of novel possibilities. This is what is apparent when Pop says "and then more and more complex," which is likewise implied in Gil's affirmation that "you can turn as many times as you like." The fact that the subject comes to consider the mode of production and its recursive nature leads logically to the substitution of the notion of indeterminacy for "many others" and of the notion of infinity in extension for some arbitrary finite number.

We have still to discuss the general problem of the relation between this constitution of infinite possibility and formal or hypothetical-deductive operations, which have as one of their characteristics the ability to reason about possibilities in which reality becomes immersed and which thus come to be interrelated by necessary links. All these behaviors we find here. The question is whether the development of formal structures explains that of the notion of possibility or whether it proceeds the other way around. Three classes of facts are relevant to this question. The most general is that procedures prepare and create structures: there is continuity between the initial analogical procedures, the deductive procedures with inferences of various types, and operational procedures at successive levels. Second, we note a similar continuity in the development and increase of varieties of possibilities, from the one or two envisioned by Pie at level IA to the infinite variety seen by Gil and Pop, as prepared by the hundreds and thousands of abstract co-possibilities characterizing level IIB: this second type of continuity certainly argues in favor of a degree of autonomy in the development of concepts of possibility. Third, the succession of qualitative varieties of possibilities, from the initial analogical forms to concrete, then abstract co-possibilities, is accompanied by the change from production of extrinsic variations without recursivity to that of intrinsic, recursive variations. This would naturally favor the development of operational structures. In short, the two types of development obviously are interrelated, but the development of the capacity to generate possibilities seems to constitute an indispensable framework for the development of operational structures.

The Car Mechanism

In the second part of the interview the car is placed in front of the subject, who is asked to make it move. The car is radio operated, and the subject is given a control with a button to be pushed to advance and to be pulled for backing up the car. There is also a steering wheel that the subject, facing it, has to turn to the left to make the car turn to the right and vice versa.

We are here not concerned with causality but with the formation of hypotheses and with the way in which subjects modify and enrich them as they attempt to try them out. We are particularly interested in possibilities including errors, and reactions to failures are of greater interest than instant successes. Of course, given the present perspective of hypothetical possibilities, it is inevitable that the behaviors observed offer a certain family resemblance to those just described.

At level IA, subjects do not perceive a problem to be solved when confronted with the steering wheel that has to be turned in the direction opposite the one the car turns when the subject is facing it. Rather, they believe that there is something wrong with the mechanism, a belief of pseudonecessity.

Yve (4;6) turns the steering wheel in the wrong direction, then simply turns the car by hand and concludes: *It doesn't work right, because I wanted to make it go this way, and it goes the other way*, which indicates his belief that the steering wheel does not function in a normal way.

Nic (4;10): *Because you turn your back on the car, it doesn't work.*

Mat (5;1), even without reversing positions, makes many errors in turning the steering wheel. He gives up, puts down the control, and only directs the car by hand.

Rob (5;5) believes the car is *perhaps out of order* but, when changing positions and seeing the car go in the expected direction, declares, pleasantly surprised, that *it's working again*. "Do you know why sometimes it moves in the right direction and sometimes not?" *no.* "Is there a trick?" *I don't think so.* "What is different, when it turns the other way?" *I don't know.*

We see that, at this initial level, an inversion is not interpreted as an objective, possible variation of identical status as a direct rotation, but rather as some kind of anomaly that upsets the normal order of events, as a twist given to a (pseudo)necessity. The error is not attributed to the subject, who broke a rule, but to the car or to its control mechanism that "doesn't work" as it should.

At the next level (naturally, with intermediate responses between levels), subjects see the unexpected outcomes as possibilities that are attributed to reality; but they make valid distinctions (and no longer simply refer to the malfunctioning of the mechanism), even if they do not succeed in understanding the problem.

Nat (6;3) first produces a number of successful moves (including a complete circle in reverse while experimenting spontaneously without predicting anything), then fails the inverted turns. "Is it possible to tell where it will go?" *No.* "What could you do to be sure?" *I don't know. Usually, when you turn the wheel toward the window, the car will go there. Sometimes it will hit the wall..* "Is this normal?" *No, it is not normal. Sometimes it turns one way, sometimes the other.* "Is it possible to turn one way and to go the other way?" *Yes, it's possible.* "How?" *I don't know.* He tries again with the car, and makes another error: *The wheels go the other way.* "Why?" *I don't know.* "Would it help to try the other side to be sure?" *Yes, it helps.*

Olg (6;6): Same errors and puzzlements. "Is it possible to know how it works?" *Yes, it is possible to know.* "Do you know?" *No.* "Some people would know?" *Yes.* "How?" *They try.*

Mic (6;11), like other subjects, succeeds in correcting his error by reversing the rotation of the steering mechanism. However, in his verbal description he says the opposite, asserting that he had turned right when in fact he had turned left, thus following what he believes should be the case and the rule.

Tia (7;1), on the other hand, succeeds after trial and error to correct his mistakes and to give a correct description of a reversal: *The car should go toward the door, so I have to turn* [the steering wheel] *toward the window.* Still, in executing his prescription he makes another error and turns the wheel in the direction of the door. He is puzzled to the point that he begins to doubt the regularities of the advance and reverse mechanism: *I hope it won't go backward when I push the button.*

Rix (7;0) neatly sums up the strategies characteristic of this level: *You never know which way to turn. You have to try it out each time.*

These reactions are comparable to those seen at level IB concerning the pathways (see above) in that they consist in analogical possibilities discovered in succession. The notion of deductible co-possibilities does not arise. What is different in this task is that the new possibilities are discovered by experimenting rather than by mental construction. What is surprising is that the subjects do not attempt to find an explanation nor even a general procedure allowing them to anticipate outcomes. Thus Olg, even though she agrees that such explanations exist—which she does not know but that others should know—can only suggest that "they try." That is, people who know would also proceed by looking for analogies.

At the next level, comparable to our level IIA (see above), we find the first signs of deduced possibilities. However, the co-possibilities, still concrete in nature, are caused by a search for an explanation of the unexpected behaviors of the automobile while manipulating the controls, and are in no way caused by predictions made by the subject:

Dan (8 years) turns the steering wheel toward the window to make the car go in that direction while he faces the car: *No, that isn't right.* "Why?" *Because it's the wrong way, the car.* "So?" *We have to turn this way* [reverse]. "And here [analogous situation]?" *The other way, too.* "And if you are in front and you want to go backward?" *The other way, too.* He succeeds six times but still commits three errors.

Jes (8;5) who has the same reactions, shows the reversals. "And if you go backward?" *That would be the same.* "Turning?" *Left* [correct]. "So?" (She turns in fact right.) "Is that correct?" *No.* This type of error occurs frequently, but it undoubtedly results from the overgeneralized use of reversals, which the subject begins to discover.

Tie (8;6) shows errors and corrections, but: *Since the car is backward, so it turns the other way.* First, however, he believes like Jes that it is *different in reverse.*

Osc (9;6) first thinks that the control effects a general reversal, contrary to *real cars where the wheels turn the same way as the steering wheel.* This causes a series of errors when the subject is not facing the car; he then discovers that *when you are behind* [at the rear of the car], *it goes there, and when you are in front, it's the other way.*

Isa (9;1), after trials and errors: "Why is it the other way?" *It's like that.* "But if you compare . . . ?" *You're in front.*

Ivo (10;4) has the same reactions. He finally concludes: *When I'm facing the other way, I have to turn differently.*

At last, at level III (almost attained by a child [9;5] classed at level IIB, who only made two errors), it only takes one trial, followed immediately by a spontaneous self-correction, for the child to find the law.

Cos (11;1): *I've turned the wrong way. To explain it, I have to go behind the car. . . . Here* [in front], *it's the opposite.*

Pop (12 years): After a single trial: *No, it's got to be the other way, because I am facing the other way than the car.*

At this level, we find the notion that one can give a causal explanation by immersing reality in a system of co-possible variations that are related to each other by necessary connections. It is easy to see why these possibilities, since they are discovered by experience, can at first be related to each other by partial laws, with errors and successes intermingled, as we saw with the level IIA notions of concrete co-possibilities. It is only at level III that we find a truly deductive notion of possibility that is apparent with the first self-correction, and this results from its integration with necessity. What is interesting about these facts—from the pseudoimpossibilities of level IA to the immediate deductive inference of level III—is the parallel development (more consistent than could have been expected) between the evolution of possibilities that are not constructed by the subject but that have to be discovered in the externally varying, real world (before they can be deduced as internal variations within a causal system); and the development of freely generated possibilities, such as those seen in the path situation.

3

The Possible Forms of
Partially Hidden Objects

with E. Marbach

Whereas in our other studies we ask the child either to arrange or construct objects in all possible ways or to solve a simple problem by any imaginable procedure—that is, in every case to imagine a potential situation not yet realized—the question we raise in this chapter concerns the way children represent the invisible portion of a partially hidden object. This implies, then, that we study possibilities not with respect to transformations to be carried out on real objects (since these are already present, even if not visible), but rather with respect to hypotheses that can be formulated concerning such objects. In this case, then, only the hypotheses are subject to modifications. We wished to find out whether, in these circumstances, we would observe the same development as in the other situations. As for the initial reactions, it seems evident that pseudonecessities limiting the number of possibilities envisioned should be reinforced by the entirely natural supposition of a complete symmetry between the visible and the invisible parts of the object. Furthermore, the fact that the invisible part already has a material existence may provide an obstacle particularly resistant to the multiplication of possibilities. This may be particularly evident in the case of a box with two circular, lateral openings from which protrude two triangular shapes, representing the extremities of the object the middle portion of which the child is asked to draw. It is interesting to observe in the 11- to 12-year-olds the same reactions we find with the construction tasks. One 12-year-old child, having drawn a diamond-shaped and a cylindrical object, replies when asked, "Can it be done another way?": "Oh yes, if one wants to take all the shapes, one can imagine any possible way." Thus, this subject views the actual shape under the screen as one particular case among an indefinite number of others that could be imagined. The problem is to see how subjects come to conceive of such co-possibilities that cannot be realized in their totality (since this is infinitely variable), having started out from an intermediate level where they already see several possibilities but only those that they could actually draw.

Method

This research uses three questions (with materials I to III). (Ia) We present a cardboard box, placed on a table, with all sides that are accessible to the child's view being of uniform color. The question concerns the sides not perceptible to the child, who is seated in front of the box. (Ib) The experimenter adds a support, which is placed under the box, of the same surface dimensions but clearly less high than the box.

(II) We present objects partly hidden in cotton: triangles and irregular-shaped objects resembling "pebbles" or "rocks," as our subjects usually call them; there are also objects of a certain structure that can be recognized from the visible portions, such as crystals and shells; finally, there is the upper part of a table tennis ball.

(III) We present a cardboard box with two triangular shapes extending at either side, which may be perceived as portions of a partially hidden object or as two independent objects. The subject is invited to explore the objects (but is given the directive not to touch them), and then a series of questions is asked. (a) The first questions concern the colors and shapes of the sides the subject cannot see. (b) The partially hidden objects are presented simultaneously or successively: "What is it like in the cotton?" "What's in the middle?" "What's at the end?" Then: "Could it be some other way?" "Do you have an idea?" "What makes you think it is like that?" "How far is it possible to go?" "How many ways do you think are there?" "How many other ways can you still see?" Another question, not always comprehended: "Is there an impossible form underneath?" The visible portions of the "pebbles" are triangular. (c) The questions are of the same kind. First, without any hint that the two ends extending from the box could be joined together, we ask the subject to imagine what is not visible and to make all possible guesses. After that we pull slightly on one side of the extending object, making the other side move and suggesting that the two ends may be parts of a single object.

Level I

For the preoperational subjects, the partially hidden object is what it is; that is, they imagine it on the basis of their immediate perception as a function of the parts that are visible (this includes the case where the child imagines an empty space between the trihedrals of question III). Although at level IB the children may hesitate between one or two possibilities, level IA children see only one: they are convinced that the only thing to do is to choose between right and wrong. They cannot conceive of having to imagine other possibilities. Here are some examples of level IA:

Phi (5;1): Question I: "Do you see all the sides?" *No.* "How many?" *Four.*

"In the back, what color is it?" *White.* "Are you sure?" *Yes.* "Could there be any other color?" *No.* "Why?" *Because the box is all white, so the back can't be another color.* "One of your friends told me it was red." *That's not true.* "Why?" *Because, if he had said that* [- if he had been right], *then that would be fine, but it isn't true.* We add the support. *That's a nice square.* "What color is it underneath?" *White.* "Could it be anything else?" *No.* Question II: He simply extends the triangle by lengthening its base (which is hidden). "Could it be another way?" *No, because it is a triangle, and a triangle always has three sides.* "Really, it couldn't be just a bit different?" *Yes, longer.* Question III: First, he thinks that the two extending triangles are two independent objects, separated by an empty space. Then, when he sees that one moves when we touch the other, he imagines a cylindrical connection. "Do you have another idea?" *Yes.* He finds a compromise between the independence and the connection of the two cones by drawing two diamonds making contact at their two pointed ends. After that, he sees no other possibilities.

Ali (5;4): I: The box is "purple," and the same color in the back. "Sure?" *Yes, because I know that all boxes are the same color on each side.* She gives the same answer for the support. II: She connects the two triangles to a common rectangular base. She completes the semicircle by drawing its symmetrical counterpart.

At sublevel IB, certain hesitations appear about pseudonecessities. But subjects do not yet imagine classes of co-possibilities. They simply begin to question whether their proposed solution is really correct or whether there could be other, more correct solutions.

Pie (6;0): I: *White* [in back]. "Could there be another color?" *Yes.* "Sure?" *No. I'm not sure.* But for the support, he guesses *red.* "But, why did you say red?" *Because I think it's red.* II: Simple extensions, except for one "rock" where he sees a possible variation, making it thicker. III: He sticks to the solution with the cylinder.

Fab (5;9), in question II, envisions two but only two different ways: enlarging the invisible part of the triangle or placing it on a base with parallel sides. After that, he discovers the possibility of combining the two: a base with one vertical, one oblique side.

Lau (6;7), in question II, cannot imagine the hidden part of the triangle: *I don't know* [what is underneath]. When we replace it by a crystal, he completes it by extension. However, he categorically rejects the idea that it could be part of a big mass hidden underneath it. *No, it's like that, I'm sure, because rock crystals are never like that.* III: He sees two possibilities—a long connection or two separate parts.

These reactions are informative as to the difficulties children have in conceiving of the notion of possibility. The principal obstacle can be characterized as follows: things in the real world being what they are, they are like that of necessity; no other possibilities exist. Since a box is usually the same color on all sides, the child sees this as a general law. Its necessity derives from a failure to distinguish facts from norms. This means that only one possibility can exist, since a necessary fact cannot be negated. All our subjects of level IA give answers just as clear as Phi's about the back of the box, and many others of levels IB and II—including Ali—start out the same way. As for the partly hidden object, since its visible portion looks regular, its invisible part must be regular in shape as well by virtue of a pseudonecessity that is analogous to the one just discussed. This explains the preponderance of solutions by simple extension or symmetry. Other solutions (such as those found at level II) are generally not envisioned, as a consequence of "pseudoimpossibilities," which are the complement of pseudonecessities.

The problem is then to explain how the child goes from this undifferentiated concept of reality=necessity=unique possibility to an open system of possibilities. One might describe this process as a dialectical one: the thesis would be that A is necessary, the antithesis A' is its negation, and the synthesis is the union of A and A' within a class B of multiple possibilities. This union is indeed the final result of the process.* The psychogenetic roots of this dialectical process of negations and progress to new systems of possibilities lie in a more general, fundamental process—the succession of equilibria, disequilibria, and reequilibria. The initial state of pseudonecessity may remain stationary for a long time depending on the problems the subject encounters, but it is prone to disequilibration for two reasons: it is a purely subjective certainty, and the subject does not actively look for reasons for justifications. This disequilibrium shows itself in a state of doubtfulness: Pie is not sure about the color—identical or different—of the back of the box, and Lau does not risk a guess as to the hidden part of the triangle. Thus, it seems clear that reequilibration in this case will consist in the subjects' admitting a multiplicity of possible shapes. This means that the disequilibrium of doubtfulness brings about a new kind of equilibrium of imagined differences. This new equilibrium comes to replace the state of pseudonecessities by a collection of co-possibilities.

At sublevel IB, which is a transitional state, we only find the beginnings of this system of co-possibilities. In fact, subjects mention only "two different ways," as Fab says (and also Lau in question III). As for Pie, when he is questioned about the color on the back of the box, he comes to conjecture with some doubt that it might be other than white, and so he proposes a different color for the support: but instead of seeing several possibilities, he decides "red" as if the nonnecessary nature of white resulted in only a single alternative possibility.

---

*This is true at all levels. An example can be found in the history of science: A=an algebra thought to be necessarily commutative (pseudonecessity), A'=negation of commutativity (Hamilton's quaternions), and B = general algebra.

Level II

From the very beginning of the concrete operational stage (and we shall have to try to explain this close synchronism), subjects discover several co-possibilities. These can be grouped in families according to their mode of generation.

Zul (7;4) functions still at level I in the case of the color of the back of the box. But in question II, she envisions three possibilities for the triangles: a big triangle of which one sees only the top, a corner of a square that is mostly hidden, and a similar corner of a rectangle. For the semicircle, she first draws a ball and then two superposed spheres of which the lower one is attached to the other at a level of about three-fourths of its height.

Mon (7;9) similarly fails with question I, but in II she completes the triangle with two kinds of bases—a linear and a semicircular one. She ends up making it look like a tip placed on a spherical body of rather irregular shape and clearly asymmetric (like the tip of a mountain flanked by foothills). As for the two ends in question III, she represents them as connected by a rod or as being equipped with segments of a rod, each of different length.

Fre (7;9) in question I imagines that the back of the box *may be* the same color as the visible parts, *but that is not sure*—it may also be red, etc. The support added, Fre gives similar responses, adding that it may also have a hole pierced through it, or it may be made of *small plates glued together of different colors*. In II, he suggests that the triangle might be taller or may have round, regular or irregular extensions. But in III, he can only suggest two separate triangles—in fact, two hidden diamond shapes symmetrical to each other.

Ben (7;11): *It's gray*, but someone may also have *colored it in back* with all sorts of colors; but for the support, she cannot envision that it may be empty. In question II, she produces 10 or so possible extensions, only one of which is of a regular form; the others become more and more irregular as she goes on. Still, she does not conclude from this that it would be possible to make them indefinitely complex. In III, Ben only thinks of regular forms, either separated like those of Fre, or connected by a point.

Cat (8;7): Question I: *That could be many different colors: white, yellow, gray, orange, pink, green, black, blue, red; there could also be different stripes.* And twice: *Inside it could be empty or full.* II: *There are several possibilities* [she draws several continuous or discontinuous forms]. *That could really be many different things.* "How many?" *Seven, 8, or 9, 10, 11, 12.*

Tie (8;0): Question I: *All possible colors, also decorations, except if there is no side to close.* In II, multiple, irregular forms. "How many different ones could there be?" *One thousand, or 100, or 200, 300, 400, 500.* "Which is closer, 1,000 or 100?" *200*[!]. In III, again, the symmetrical object leads back to regularity: two triangles either separated or connected by a thin bar or a rectangle.

Fel (9;6), in question I: *It's gray.* "Could it be another way?" *Yes — green, purple, blue, white, yellow. That's all.* The support: *It's the same. But there could be a hole.* In II, a mixture of regular and other shapes. But in III — after several symmetrical forms, separated or joined, among them a horizontally placed diamond shape — a lance shape with two unequal points.

Bir (9;0) can see well all the possibilities in question I, including *an opening on the bottom* [of the box itself] *or several*; also, *all possible colors.* But it is curious that still at her age she conceives of all the co-possibilities not as simultaneously coexisting in the abstract but only as concrete, successive actualizations: *Oh yes, if you put up a different box. . . . If I close my eyes every time you put on a new color.* Question II yields the same kinds of reactions as given by the other subjects; but in III, after a few regular-shaped junctions, Bir goes on to imagine some zigzaggy ones and some irregularly curved ones.

Lai (10;0): *Any color. Perhaps there's nothing in back.*

These reactions raise a number of problems, the first being how to explain the change from level IB, with its limitation of two possibilities, to the increasing number observed here. However, this number is still not very high, even for the "rocks" (which Tie limits at 200), which is a far cry from the indeterminate infinity characteristic of level III. The developmental process certainly has something to do with the absence of arguments justifying the limitation to only two possibilities. As long as subjects limit themselves to only one possibility (level IA), they find justification in the pseudonecessities invoked to that end. But two and "only two," as Fab says, cannot be explained unless they are in a relation of negation to each other: A and not-A. But we are dealing here not with negations but with differences, and each difference can evoke another one by combination or variation (Fab derives from his "only two different ways" a combination of the two). In short, the discovery of two procedures breeds doubt ("Why only two?"), and this disequilibrium provides a push toward reequilibration that incites the subject to look for other transformations.

The mechanism of this reequilibration by making new possibilities available is related to the type of transfer characteristic of procedures. The transfer from the first procedure to a second one (level IB) constitutes a beginning that will lead to further transfers at level II. This kind of transfer is different from operational generalization (even the simple extensional kind), which consists in subordinating an earlier system to another, more general one, of which the older system remains a subsystem. The transfer of procedures is, in fact, transversal in that it proceeds by analogies — that is, by making use of similarities (as correspondences) but without neglecting the differences, which, in fact, have to be discovered. Transfers operate in a way like categorial functors, but without the "forgetting" dimension, since (on the contrary) new possibilities need to be uncovered that are different from the previously known ones.

As new procedures come to be added by transverse analogies and not by inclusion, these transfers remain open and, moreover, depend on each other. Therefore, it is inevitable that, once a particular transfer has taken place (such as that between the two possibilities at level IB), it entails new transfers, which generate not classes (at least not immediately)—since there is no subordination—but what we shall call *families* of new openings and possibilities. For example, having transformed the angle perceived in question II into the top of a large triangle, Zul proceeds thence to make a corner of a square, and then of a rectangle. Ben links this angle to a nontriangular figure, which she then transforms into more and more irregular shapes. But, in keeping with the analogical nature of transfers, the triangles in question II lend themselves well to the production of more and more different possibilities; those placed at opposite ends in question III, however, continue for a long time to exert a pressure toward symmetry, which explains the regularity of the joints proposed by our subjects, from Mon to Pie. Only the 9-year-old subjects (Fel and Bir) show transfers from levels II to III by producing symmetrical joints and even irregular shapes in question III.

In short, it is on the basis of analogies that procedural transfers are an open-ended source of ever new possibilities, for, as a conjunct of similarities and differences, the analogy between A and B is followed by another between B and C, and another between C and D, without clear analogies between A and C or D. In the absence of class inclusion or seriation, the successive analogies remain devoid of any kind of recursiveness. If on occasion a procedure involves a goal direction, this precursive character does not affect the analogies as such, in spite of the fact that the search is directed by it (but only as by a tendency). Thus, the system of procedural transfers is in a constant state of disequilibrium; or one might say that it characterizes an equilibration process in evolution, which is essentially incomplete until level III, where we find a state of relative completion. But to understand its precise nature, we have to first attempt to explain the limitations characteristic of level II.

In fact, their cause is easy to see. Level IA showed a complete lack of differentiation between reality, necessity, and possibility. By comparison, level II marks a beginning differentiation, but with one limitation (which is not surprising, given the period of concrete operations): that the possibilities accessible to the subjects remain concrete also, that they can all be realized by actions carried out by a material subject of flesh and bone. Level III subjects, who are 11 to 12 years old, will talk about "infinity," no longer depending on material actions but rather on the subjects' deductive capacities; whereas Fel in question I enumerates six colors and concludes, "That's all." Bir (also 9 years old) does speak of "all" colors, but she adds that those colors would have to be painted on the box, one after the other, by the experimenter, while she would "close my eyes every time." This is indeed a far cry from formal generalization! Tie asserts that he has seen "pebbles of all shapes," but he limits them to 200 possibilities, which certainly is progress compared with Lau's refusal (at level IB), but remains modest when compared with infinity.

This leads us back to our usual problem: Is it the case that the limitations inherent in these families of possibilities being dependent on material realizations are responsible for the concrete operations of this level, or is it the concrete nature of these operations that slows progress in the development of possibilities? There are three reasons for choosing the former interpretation. First, the analogies and procedural transfers are more general and appear earlier in development than do operations: in some situations, they may already be apparent at the sensorimotor level. Second, families of co-possibilities arise essentially from recognition of similarities and differences, whereas operational structures require, in addition, a precise equilibrium between positive and negative statements of various types. And third, it seems that the process leading from an initial state of undifferentiated perceptions of the three modes—reality, possibility, and necessity—to more and more differentiated concepts (and finally to an integration of the three) is much more general and all-pervasive than is the development of logical operations; therefore, it seems that it is this overall development that determines the operational structures.

Level III

Around 11 or 12 years of age, one observes a kind of sudden mutation that leads abruptly to the notion of infinite numbers of possibilities after a few concrete, limited co-possibilities of the level II variety.

Pat (10;7), at first, in question II, seems to proceed by rather restricted variations that are, however, distinguished by suggesting the possibility of continuity; with the "pebbles," he proceeds by extensions: *It could go all the way down or may be shorter, perhaps halfway down to the bottom.* "Why do you say 'perhaps'?" *Because the pebbles may have any kind of shape.* (To the suggestion that the crystal may be part of a larger mass, an idea rejected by Lau at level IB, he says: *If it is sat on a rock, yes*). The semicircle he first completes by a circle, then sections it. After two sections, he says: *There could be smaller ones, if one cuts up higher . . . up to infinity*[!].

Ber (11;0), having produced two or three minor variations on question II according to length, width, and curvature, says, *You haven't done very many, just enough to stimulate our imagination. . . . Let's suppose that this represents all shapes*; in each case, he repeats, *That may be any kind of shape.*

Cla (11;3), in question II: *That could be any form as long as there is a tip that stands out and that one can see.* The same reactions in question III with rectilinear and curved designs.

Ano (11;2): Question II: *Any kind of form as long as the ends that stick out are triangles. The rest is not important* [=could be anything], *since it can't be seen.*

Sam (11;10): *One cannot tell: an indefinite shape.*

Arl (12;0): *One can imagine all possible shapes.*

This apparently sudden change from possibilities that are realizable by analogical transfers to ones that are deduced and immediately generalized to indefinite and infinite possibilities presents a certain interest and calls for explanation. Let us first recall the role of analogy as an endogenous principle of procedural transfers, and thus of the generation of new possibilities. Given a particular starting procedure for solving a specific problem (here the drawing of a half-hidden object), subjects might ask themselves whether there are better ones or simply different ones. In our experiments, we solicit these questions; but in everyday life, initial procedures resulting from trial and error and the equilibrium between the subject's schema and the adjustments required by the data must be ascertained as well as they can be, so there is constant questioning. If the new attempt is too similar to the previous ones, it adds nothing new. If it is too different, it is not likely to be immediately obvious. Thus, the only way accessible is that of analogies, which are neither simple equalities nor pure differences, but a coordination of the two. Here new possibilities are all the easier to conceive because successive analogies are nonrecursive: B can be analogous to A with respect to characteristic x; C can be to B with respect to y (common to B and C) but not x (not present in C); so there is no analogy between A and C, even though A has led to C by way of B. It is by means of this kind of analogical process that the concrete possibilities of level II are generated in problems not calling for operational solutions. How can we explain, then, that at level III these same problems produce deductive procedures, even to a point where subjects think in terms of "any kind" of possibilities (Ber and Cla, etc.) and of "infinite" or "indefinite" ones (Pat and Sam)?

To return to analogy (in which, as we have seen, there is always a difference behind each similarity and vice versa), two new elements appear even in Pat's reactions: first, the variations proposed are all directed toward *more* or *less* (longer and longer or shorter and shorter, etc.); second, between the discontinuous states that subjects envision, they imagine a continuum of an infinite number of intermediate states. Compared with analogy, this two-way quantification implies that the relations between similarities and differences do not change with the linear succession of simple external variations, but rather become organized in a recursive system of internally represented variations. As a result, even invisible differences — not to say infinitesimal ones — can be perceived behind the graded similarities. In other studies, subjects readily identified even totally imperceptible similarities disguised under varying degrees of transformations.*

---

*See chapter 8 where 11-year-old subjects, given the task of building the biggest pile using the same blocks, recognize that there is conservation of volume whichever way the blocks are arranged.

These general properties are the ones that characterize the formal operational stage. Another study concerning invisible differences is that of the bar moved by imperceptibly minute propulsions so that its displacement can only be seen after several replications. Here, too, 11-year-olds do not, like younger subjects, cling to their perceptions; but they say, for instance, "Maybe it moves just a bit [right from the start], otherwise it would never move." Similarly, they will deduce by pure inference without resorting to observation or measurement that each action produces an equivalent reaction, when they are confronted with a situation where similarities are to be postulated under apparent differences.

This brings us back to our problem of level II: Is it the case that the development of operational structures brings about the observed progressions in openness to new possibilities, or is it rather the other way around? Only two things can be said here about this point. First, since, as we believe, the development of operations is caused by a mechanism of equilibrations and self-adjustments, we must also postulate some kind of regulatory process in the formation of possibilities. This regulatory process manifests itself in the interplay of similarities and differences and their equilibration in the constitution of families of co-possibilities, as well as in the progress toward mental representations of recursive changes. Hence, since any kind of regulatory process concerns possible variations, it follows that the regulation of possibilities and the possibilities inherent in the regulations that give rise to operations must be part of a general system of equilibration—an inclusive, global mechanism. Second, we must take into account the development of the notion of necessity (which will be studied in another volume), which is subject to a general law of equilibration as specified at the end of level II: initial nondifferentiation between reality, possibility, and necessity (pseudonecessities), followed by progressive differentiation and, finally, at level III, subordination of reality to the necessary relationships between possibilities: in other words, equilibrium between differentiations and integrations. If this is so, it is obvious that by merging the development of operational structures with a general process that is itself part of a mechanism of equilibration, the results of our earlier analyses are in no way contradicted by this assumption. However, it remains to be demonstrated how such regulations in procedural analogies come about, in the sense of stable groupings of similarities and differences, and particularly how the latter achieve their final form through the organization of negations, which are still dependent on particular contents at the level (II) of concrete operations but which achieve a purely formal character when possibilities become coordinated by means of necessary links.

4

Sectioning a Square

with E. Marti and C. Coll

We decided to observe a behavior as ordinary as that of sectioning paper to compare the formation of possibilities in two situations—one without problems, the other with predetermined questions. In the former, we present children with a number of cardboard squares measuring 7 cm², the only instruction being to cut them in "any way you like" and to use the cutout pieces to cover up an orange square, also measuring 7 cm² (glued to an irregular surface), after having placed the white square over the orange square and noted their equality in size. Even though this equality constitutes a certain constraint, it presents no problem to the subjects. It only helps us to see how they construe the relations between the "pieces" and the whole. In addition, we present two kinds of problems: (a) cut the square into two, three, or four pieces in all possible ways and (b) divide the square into two, three, or four equal parts, which raises questions concerning number and size, as will be shown below.

Free cutting: Levels IA and IB

The only possibilities perceived at this initial level are of the kind that attribute a specific meaning to the pieces—that is, a meaning that sets them apart from the whole, from the cardboard square to be cut. Let us note at once that these "pieces" or "parts," unrelated to the whole, cannot be explained with reference to the semantics of expressions like "a piece of music" or "a pleasure party"* to designate specific and self-sufficient members of a set or a genre. The reactions of level IA subjects reveal problems of quite a different sort arising from difficul-

---

Translator's note: The French original has *une partie de ballon*, which literally means *a ball game*. To preserve the relation to *part* evident in the French expression, the translator chose the term *pleasure party*, which resembles the French expression phonetically, semantically, and etymologically even though the word *party* no longer conveys the sense of *part*, as does the French *partie*.

39

ties with class inclusion (in this case spatial) of the kind we observed back in 1921, when we saw children assimilate the sense of expressions like "part of [or some of] my flowers" to that of "my few flowers." So we obtain interchanges like these: "What is a part?" *It's something cut off.* "And the other part?" *There isn't any more*[!]. Here are two examples:

Nic (5;5), having verified the equality of the orange square and having received the instruction to cover it with pieces cut out of the white square, cuts out a square smaller than the original square. "How many pieces are there?" *One.* "What is it called?" *A square also.* "Can you cover the orange square?" She puts down her small square. "And that [the rest], what can we do with that?" *We can put it down too.* "Is it a piece too?" *No, it's not a piece.* "Can you think of something else?" She cuts another small triangle out of the white cardboard. *A triangle!* "How many pieces are there?" *One.* "Can you cover the orange board?" *It's too small . . . We put down the other end* [note the neutral term!] "Still another idea?" She cuts out: *A rectangle.* "Can you cover it?" *Still too small, I'll put down the leftover.* "There are how many pieces [we point to all of them]?" *One again* [= as before]. "Still another idea?" *A round one* [the same reactions]. "Still more?" *No, I can't think of any others.*

Pat (5;0) at first cuts out only shapes with concrete meanings (contrary to Nic's spatial forms): feet, letters (*P* and *T*), *two wheels* for a truck (*It's easy to do a round one*), *a thing to make screws tight* (a screwdriver). When we ask him to cover up the orange surface, he answers: *In any case, I know how*; but when asked, "How many pieces?" *No, that* [the remainder], *that's nothing, the others that's nothing too*; only the meaningful pieces count. He then cuts out a leg and a foot. He places all his cutouts on the orange surface, four in all, but he counts only two. When asked to do only two pieces, however, he cuts the square into 10 parallel strips, counting up to five, saying, *The other ones aren't* [pieces].

These and similar reactions, which can be found mixed in with others up until 6 or even 7 years of age, clearly signify that for these subjects to cut up a square with scissors does not mean to divide it up into parts and to distribute these so that they can be reassembled on the orange square in a way equivalent to their initial state. The action of cutting the square generates only one general procedure (in spite of the diversity and variability of expressions): to take out of this whole whatever is needed to make the shapes representing empirical or spatial contents. These lose all relation to the whole, which ceases to exist as such; it gets destroyed and only some "ends and leftovers" remain (Nic). Pat even goes so far as to say "that's nothing," although he is able to use these bits to cover up the orange square ("In any case, I know how"), but he perceives them as indexes of the initial whole conserved.

Several intermediate, mixed reactions can be grouped as belonging to level IB. Some of these are identical with those just described, and others begin to show signs of a new kind of possibilities: that of cutouts as partitions. Yet, although the remainder is here counted as a part of a whole, it is not on a par with the others, thus still enjoying special status.

Rez (5;10) cuts out *a triangle*, then two triangles joined together at an angle, which she calls a *bow tie*, then a *ball*, *a snowman*, *a globe*, *a house*, *a bed*, *a fountain with a top there*, etc. When covering the orange square with the parts (the triangle and the remainder), she says: *There are three, because with the orange it makes three.* But on the last trial, she counts only two: the fountain and the top. "What about that [the remainder]?" *I don't know.* This is still far from the whole-part concept.

Mur (5;5) similarly counts as three a triangle and its remainder, an oval, and what remains when placing them on the orange square. But, having divided the square into three equal strips, she counts two pieces, neglecting the part that remains as if the two cutout pieces were of a different kind.

Kat (6;7), having cut out four narrow strips around the edges of the square, counts correctly five pieces; but for two strips, she declares having cut the square into only *two parts*, neglecting to count the big center piece. Then she cuts out six triangles, then four circles, which she labels *Cat faces*. "How many pieces?" *Four . . . five.* "Four or five?" *Four.* "How many altogether?" *There are four cut out* [she points to the four holes in the white square] *and there's one square inside* [= the remainder].

Ari (7;0) cuts out a circle, then the four corners of the square (counting only four pieces); then a half circle, two triangles, and two strips, which makes *five pieces*. "With those five, can one cover the orange square?" *No, we have to use that too* [the remainder]. "Why didn't you count it?" *Because it is not small.*

Isa (6;0) starts out as at level II with a complete division of the square, counting the pieces correctly. But to cover the orange square, she cannot see the possibility of putting the pieces back together to remake the original whole; so she cuts 12 very small squares out of the white square, which she puts onto the orange square in discontinuous fashion. She does not know what to do with the large remainder: *There's no more place.*

Cat (6;1) cuts out a rectangle, then a half circle, then two irregular shapes joined together, etc.; she counts only these, because *the other pieces* [the remainder] *are not so important*[!]. Having to cover the orange square, she only uses four out of her five pieces. When she notes that *no, there's still some orange showing*, she picks up another white square and cuts out 12 tiny squares, which she places on the square with no contiguity between them. She finally gives up, not knowing what to do with the rest.

Rol (7;6) cuts out four pieces (*an igloo, a ball, a cloud* and *a square*), but she counts four and not five. "What about that [the remainder]?" *Five, it makes, yes, it's a piece too.* "Just like the others?" *No, there are holes all over.* Also, she is unable to cover up the surface of the orange square in a situation with four regular shapes and an irregular remainder.

The new trend to perceive the remainder as another piece prefigures a new possibility, which is to conceive of the action of cutting as of a division into parts. Still, each of the cases presented remains rather far from this new level, since some do not see the whole as a piece except for the orange square (Rez and Mur); for others, the remaining piece has a different status (Mur, Kat, and Ari). Most important, subjects do not see the equivalence between the pieces put back together and the whole (Isa, Cat, and Rol are unable to complete the task of covering up the orange square).

One exceptional case is worth mentioning, remarkable in its precociousness. This case allows us to witness the genesis of the new possibility of proceeding by partitioning or by division of the square without leaving any remainder considered as such. The reason this case is not classified as level II, even though he attains it, is that generally he does not use the square in his partitioning, his only ambition being to make "big," "medium," and "small pieces":

Jer (5;0) starts out with a surprising, analogical series by cutting off four ends along the four borders until he ends up with a square piece so small that it is practically impossible to cut any further: *Before, this was a square.* "And now?" *Small pieces.* "Can you think of another way?" *Big pieces.* He divides the square up into eight irregular shapes, cutting in curved and in straight lines in any direction. "Good. Another way?" *Medium ones.* Same procedure, only ending up with six pieces, of which he does not see that they are larger than his "big" ones. "And still another way?" This time he uses median lines as at level II, then an irregular partition into four pieces. *I've cut them big.* "Another way?" Two cuts followed by six parallel, horizontal cuts. *I've cut them real tiny.* Then he returns to his initial idea of cutting along the four borders. He places everything on the orange square. "That makes how many pieces?" *Five.* "Show them." He indicates eight points in succession along the circumference—not, in fact, separated, amounting to a virtual cutout. *There are eight.* "But for covering up the orange square?" *One, two, three* [he actually cuts these out]. . . . *I covered it!*"

It can be seen how subjects stop trying to construct shapes with qualitative meanings, either empirical (shapes of particular objects) or spatial, and how they attempt instead to create pieces that simply differ in size (small, medium, and large). This leads them to give up the procedure of taking off individual pieces, which leaves them always with an unidentified remainder. We've seen how from there, subjects discover a new procedure, that of simple partitioning. This in turn leads to a new conceptualization of relations between the parts and the whole, which now comes to be perceived as the reunion of parts and nothing more. What is interesting about level I (A and B) is the long and laborious process by which subjects come to discover this new possibility, whereas the idea of partitions might have imposed itself from the beginning (as it does, in fact, in other situations: see chapter 5).

Free Cutting: Levels II and III

Level II is thus characterized by the procedure of partitioning, which proceeds from the whole to arrive at the parts; whereas that of separating proceeds from the parts in order to try, with difficulty, to relate these to the inevitable residue. It is not surprising that in this particular situation, which makes use of a square form, subjects will use this regular shape in their initial partitions. This explains the role symmetry plays initially in acquisitions; other combinations and variations appear somewhat later at varying time intervals. Here are some examples:

Bel (6;5) divides the square in two: first vertically, then horizontally. "Is it different?" *Yes, in direction.* "Other ways?" A diagonal, then the other. *That makes four pieces.* Then she adds more diagonals and the medians. *That makes eight pieces.* "How did you figure this?" *It's that I could make two more lines.* Then she does a diagonal and a median to make four pieces, then two diagonals with a small circle in the center; a simple circle in the middle; both medians (not yet done); a quarter of a circle in each corner and a circle in the center; five small circles in the same places, etc. Then we have her cut out a large circle, and she finds the symmetries of up to eight equidistant radii.

Pie (7;4) divides immediately into four and each quarter again into four, making 16 small squares. But since his cutting was imprecise, he has difficulty covering up the orange square without allowing certain irregularities. "Do you think that might make a square bigger than the white one?" *No, because before it was the same.* Then he does six different combinations using the medians and diagonals; then two configurations of three triangles, which cover the whole piece; then a figure with a complete diagonal, which cuts through one of the quarters (creating two half medians). "Still another idea, a very different one?" He cuts six pieces, three equal pairs. With a circle he imagines zigzags and complex detours after a few initial symmetries.

Rik (7;6) produces 20 or so combinations similar to those of Pie but including cuttings parallel to the diagonals; small triangles cut out at each corner of the square and from the middle; vertical cuts dividing the square into three and four parts with horizontal crossings (16 combinations of this last model); as well as complex, symmetrical and asymmetric nestings.

Ros (7;6), in addition to straight-line cuttings, including a series of continuous small squares and triangles, cuts out curvilinear, asymmetric shapes similar to those of level I—for example, four irregular shapes, which she calls *clouds.* When asked how many pieces that makes, she counts from 1 to 12, then counting to 8 while looking at the rest. "How does that make 12? Over there, there are only 4." *I've done it in my head.* She meant to say that the "rest" that was not cut out contains 8 potential pieces to be added to those already cut.

Gin (8;1), after a series of straight-line cuttings, cuts out a single round piece in the center of the square. "How many pieces are there?" He counts four potential pieces in the residue, like Ros. "How are we going to count these two [the round piece and the rest]?" *Two parts*. On a large circle he stays with symmetrical shapes but produces one permutation: two half circles, first touching at their bases and then turned around.

Fer (8;2) first divides the square in two, then into four parts, then cuts each half into eight horizontal strips and each quarter into 12 small squares of equal size. Then he goes on to asymmetric combinations: three of the quarters get divided into units, while the last one stays intact. Further, the whole square gets divided up by 20 oblique lines, close together and running parallel to the diagonal. Finally, some triangles are cut in the corners or along the sides, and some symmetrical curves.

Man (8;4) and Rom (8;9) produce a large number of asymmetric shapes. Rom, for example, divides the square into four unequal parts, such as a quarter of a circle and different patterns within each piece.

Ana (9;0), in addition to the above, invents a variety of "wave" shapes and zigzags.

These examples suffice to show how asymmetric and symmetrical variations are multiplied when the new procedure consisting of partitioning the square leads to a whole new series of goals. But contrary to what we find with the constrained task, we do not observe a clear dividing line between symmetrical and asymmetric partitions, even though the latter become relatively more frequent with age and the increasing inventiveness shown by the subjects. We shall return to this topic of the different ways new possibilities emerge from earlier ones after we examine the bipartite and tripartite divisions. We shall also take up again the question of the relationship between symmetrical and asymmetric divisions.

Let us finally cite one or two cases of level III, which is marked by the discovery of recursive variations capable of infinite extension:

Val (9;9), after a few initial asymmetric divisions, comes to produce *a cross* to connect the sides opposite each other, and from there goes on to a system of nested forms that can lead to *thousands* of cuttings.

Jea (10;7), after a large number of divisions, for which he already uses recursive methods (such as a series of seven squares containing from two *to eight parts*, similarly goes on to produce nestings by successive cuttings along three sides of the square, where he produces nested rectangles — *no two being of exactly the same size. Each time it gets a bit smaller*.

These are typical reactions at this level.

Bipartitioning the Square

Following the free cutting, the subjects were asked to cut the square the way they wish but in such a way that in the end there should be exactly two pieces. This task as formulated suggests partitioning rather than simply separation of pieces.

Furthermore, after the first question, we asked that the two pieces be exactly equal. Thus both questions involve predetermined procedures rather than free choices, and we wanted to compare the two methods and their results in relation to their capacity to reveal the formation of possibilities. In particular, although this second method produces quite comparable results as to general development processes, there are individual differences in the respective levels revealed by the two methods.

Level IA again manifests itself in strategies leaving unusable residues:

Jer (5;0), whose exceptional precociousness in regard to the procedure of complete partitioning we discussed above, regresses to the more primitive strategy of separating isolated parts when confronted with the task to produce dichotomies: "Now, we shall play at cutting the square into two pieces only." He cuts an arc of a circle with a triangle on top. *That's a house for a snail.* "Now, do two pieces of equal size." Two arcs of a circle, one on top of the other. *That's one and two.* "I have an idea too [we cut the square at its vertical midline]. "Do you like this?" *Yes, that's two pieces.* "Another idea?" He cuts two quadrilateral parts without bothering about the remainder.

Pat (5;0), as already noted, has cut 10 pieces, of which he retains 5 in response to our request for "two pieces only." "I had asked for two, not five." *There* [he cuts out two vertical strips and puts them horizontally on the orange square]. "That makes how many pieces?" *Two.* "And that [the remainder]?" *No.*

Cat (6;1) cuts the square in half along a midline; but instead of leaving it at that she cuts one of the halves into two further halves and offers the two quarters as the two pieces requested.

Rol (7;0) cuts out a small circle and a small quadrilateral. "How many pieces?" *Two.* "But we don't want any leftovers." So she divides the square into two very unequal rectangles and keeps the bigger one in her hand. *It doesn't come out without a leftover.* "Can you explain?" *When one cuts, there is always the leftover to make two pieces. Otherwise you can only make a big one like that.** We had not asked for equal sizes.

In these subjects, a procedure requiring an exhaustive partitioning remains at the level of incomplete subtraction, even in subjects like Jer, who in the free cutting procedure had successfully performed exhaustive partitions. At level IB, we find subjects who still proceed by subtractions but who take the residue as a valid part; they may even perform spontaneous partitionings.

Nic (5;5), who was seen to give typical level IA reactions (*the rest is not a piece*), as soon as she is asked for two pieces cuts the square into two unequal rectangles. Then she cuts another one in half, dividing the square along a vertical midline. But when she is asked for two equal pieces, she cuts out two small triangles without noticing that she had just before successfully solved the problem.

---

*It will be recalled that Ari (7;0) had stipulated (above) that "a piece" must be "small".

Mur (5;5) cuts out *a car* (with eight sides!) and says spontaneously that that makes two (with the rest). The same reactions with *a house* and *a tree* together with the remainders. But when asked to do two equal ones, there appear some strange fluctuations: she correctly produces two halves but is not satisfied with that solution, so she cuts out of one of the halves two small triangles and concludes: *That's it*. After this, again two halves (through the midline), and this time they seem satisfactory to her; then she produces two halves by cutting along one diagonal and repeats this with the other.

Rez (5;10) similarly cuts out *a house*, then *a bed*, etc., each time counting two pieces together with the rest. For equality, she cuts along a diagonal, then along a midline. Then she returns to simple cutouts by subtraction.

Kat (6;7) cuts out a form with three curvatures. *There, that's two parts: one piece and the other is saved*. Four similar reactions follow, with increasing amounts of irregularity. When asked to do two equal parts, she divides the lower end of the square into five or six units (by moving the scissors), but she does not count them. Instead she sections the square starting from the middle division by cutting along the vertical midline. After this, she continues like this, always starting out by dividing the lower end of the square then cutting at about the midline (but getting less precise as she goes along), doing zigzags and getting more irregular in dividing the square into what she believes are two equal parts. She admits at most being *off just a bit* (pointing toward the left side) while cutting from the bottom to the top.

Compared with the preceding subjects, whose performance with the constrained task did not produce better results than the free cutting task and even produced inferior results in some cases (Jer), there is clear progress with the subjects just described, who were of the same ages. The dichotomy is now understood as exhaustive partitioning, even where subjects perform cutouts with a remainder. However, when asked to produce two equal parts, Nic only produces partial cutouts, and Mur and Rez mix these with exact and symmetrical bipartitions. Kat's responses are extraordinary with their measures at the base of the square, their selection of the midline to produce two halves, and then their successive departures from this line in the direction of increasing inequalities and erratic lines. This illustrates well the multiplicity of possibilities made available by the combination of the procedures used to solve a problem that delimits them.

At level II, where the free cutting follows a procedure of partitioning and no longer of subtracting, it is to be expected that dichotomies and bipartitions should be facilitated. Yet, whereas the reactions described above show no break between symmetrical and asymmetric cuttings, the present task leads to a level IIA, which is distinguished from IIB by the fact that dichotomies are only successfully produced along axes of symmetry whereas at level IB they can also be achieved asymmetrically. Here are a few examples of level IIA:

Bel (6;5) obtains dichotomies by cutting the square along its medians and diagonals. "Can you do it another way?" *Yes.* She cuts two strips along opposite
sides. *One and two pieces. No, that will make three pieces.* "So, is there another
way?" *Yes, that one* [vertical midline], *but we've already done that one.* She cannot find another possibility.

Nat (7;4): *I'm thinking of that one* [median]. *There are many ideas with two
pieces.* But once she's cut a bit to the left of the midline, she does the same thing
on the right. *That would make two pieces. Ah! . . . three! I'll cut only there*
[median].

Mar (7;6) also only finds divisions along axes, then she cuts out two equal
small triangles: *Two . . . ah! three!*

Yet Nat and Mar had already produced asymmetric dichotomies in the free
cutting task (an angle at a corner or a circle not in the center, while explicitly
counting "two pieces"). Now that they are asked to cut the square in two, they
regress back to symmetrical cuts, as if the addition of a constraint prevents the
subjects from bringing to the fore what they had already achieved when the only
aim was to produce something novel: there is thus a similar regression in the
constrained task for level IIA as had been observed at level IA. At level IIB,
however, we observe the opposite trend:

Ros (7;6), after a few symmetries, cuts a narrow angle at a corner of the
square: *You do a small one like that and you leave* [=keep] *the big one.* Then
a strip at an angle, ⌐ , plus the remainder, a star, and the rest, etc. When asked
to produce two halves, she returns to symmetries.

Rik (7;6), who had produced a rich variety of both symmetrical and asymmetric patterns in the free cutting situation but no dichotomies other than symmetrical ones, begins by cutting along the axes but soon goes on to produce a
small triangle, a small square in different positions, more triangles of different
shapes, etc., each time counting *two* including the remainder.

Fer (8;2), who in the free cutting task had produced only one dichotomy
through the midline, finds many asymmetric ones in the structured task—some
similar to Rik's, others with curved lines.

Ana (9;6) first does some partitions along midlines and diagonals, then cuts
the square from one angle to its opposite using many different paths of curvilinear or zigzag shape.

The structured task thus leads to important increases in the number of possibilities, which subjects had simply not thought of in the free cutting situation,
as they become eager to go on to patterns more interesting than dichotomies.
The only new reaction observed for level III is that, when asked to cut out two
pieces of equal size, subjects do not restrict themselves to symmetries as they
do at level IIB but succeed in constructing equal surfaces with angular or curved
lines by compensation along the cut:

Val (9;9) first cuts the square along midlines and diagonals: *There are just four ways, or maybe there are more, but it's hard to do. I have a bit of an idea how to do it.* She cuts down from the top edge at the middle to the bottom edge, using three straight-line segments between which she inserts two semicircular shapes of opposite orientation. *There are two round ones that are the same, the middle, too. Here it's the same.* One recalls her "thousands" of cuts possible (above).

Cel (11;4), after many dichotomies, when asked to do "two pieces of the same size," says, *That's easy* [the midline or the diagonal]. "Any others?" *That's much harder.* He replaces the diagonal by a wavy line that is well balanced in its turns, then by a zigzag with two equal angles—one on the left, the other on the right.

We return to this problem in the next chapter.

Tripartitions

Dividing into three pieces shows conclusively how the procedures of subtracting and partitioning are different from each other. As for the former, there are no problems:

Nic (5;5), when asked to cut the square into three pieces, cuts out three small squares, then three small triangles.

Jer (5;0) (see above, where he succeeds in partitioning and then later regresses to subtraction) cuts out a house, its roof, and the *front door, that makes three.*

At level IIA, however, subjects go so far as to deny the possibility of trichotomy, independently even of the equalization of the three parts:

Bel (6;5), having produced dichotomies only by symmetry, when asked to do three pieces, says, *No, that is not possible.* "Think about it." *There aren't three.* "Why?" *Because like this* [the median] *there are two and like that* [two medians] *there are four pieces.* And she forgets that just a little while before she had cut out two lateral strips in the belief that she would obtain two pieces and had concluded by herself: *No, that would make three.*

Mar (7;6) understands well that by cutting one strip, then two, then three it is possible to obtain three cutouts, but she aims for exhaustive partition and finds that she has four pieces instead of three. Like Bel she forgets that she has previously obtained three by cutting out two small triangles. She cannot comprehend, like many other subjects, that with n cuts one obtains $n+1$ parts.

With the asymmetric dichotomies of level IIB, tripartitions are mastered but equalization remains problematic:

Fer (8;2): *With three, that's hard, I can't do it.* "Why?" *Now, I know* [he divides into two with a diagonal, then divides one of the halves into two again]: *Ah, yes, one, two, three.*

Ani (9;9) divides into three with ease, using a horizontal and cutting the rest vertically, etc. But for three equal parts, *It's impossible, it can't be done because it's not big enough or not small enough.* "With a different shape you could do it?" *Yes, with a rectangle, that is longer, so one could do equal parts* [does it]. "Good, and with the square?" Instead of using the same procedure, she attempts three triangles. *No.*

Pie (10;7) quickly produces five examples of trichotomies using straight or curved lines, but when asked to do three equal parts he only succeeds in producing cutouts and *there is always* a remainder to make four.

At level III there no longer is any problem:

Cel (11;4): Dividing into three: *That's easy* (he offers spontaneously three equal parts on the square).

These problems with tripartitions, already studied quite some time ago with B. Inhelder, are interesting from the point of view of possibility because they reveal initial pseudonecessities limiting their formation and the emergence of later pseudonecessities at all levels of development—such as the symmetry restriction observed at level II—that are just as limiting.

As for quadripartitions, they do not pose any new problems compared with bipartitions except that subjects sometimes have difficulty predicting that four cuts make five parts and not four, just as in trichotomies children usually expect to get three pieces with three cuts and do not understand the necessary relation "n cuts $\supset n+1$ parts" (see Mar).

Conclusions

The crucial development in this task is that by 7–8 years of age children give up the subtraction procedure in favor of partitioning. This is also the average age for the formation of partitive operations (the infralogical equivalent of logico-arithmetical class inclusion). So the question is, as usual, whether it is these operations that generate the new possibilities or whether it is the other way around. To answer this question, we may consider the interesting example of Jer (5;0), who, on the one hand, characterizes his pieces in terms of size, thus rendering them homogeneous with the remainder and achieving exhaustive partitioning. But, on the other hand, this focusing on size and the resulting partitioning do not suffice to distinguish extension (number of parts) from intension (size as a property):* thus, he believes that eight pieces are "bigger" than six "medium ones," as if it were not the case that the number of parts is inversely related to their size. And when asked to do dichotomies, he regresses to the more primitive subtraction procedure. Cases like these show that partitioning as a procedural possibility predates operational partitions. This is also confirmed by the cases

---

*In our earlier studies with B. Inhelder (*The Early Growth of Logic in the Child: Classification and Seriation* [New York: Harper and Row, 1964]), we stressed this initial lack of differentiation between extension and intension.

of level IB when bipartitioning the square, which remain clearly preoperational, only achieving exhaustive partitioning when extension is specifically mentioned in the instruction.

This development of possibilities toward logical operations raises the general problem of the way new possibilities become available at each successive level and how they are related to the process of equilibration. Looked at from this angle, the characteristics of level I are simultaneously a deficiency (subjects see no relation between the parts and the whole), a pseudonecessity deriving from this deficiency (the necessity to confer an independent meaning on these pieces), and, finally, a pseudoimpossibility resulting from both of the preceding characteristics (the failure to utilize the "rest" as another "piece," since it is no longer a part of the whole and thus has no meaning); hence, there are three kinds of limitations. Yet within this limited field of possibilities, there exists a way to open up possibilities that is, in principle, quite general: each possibility once realized can lead on to another by analogy or (more or less) free association. If the meaning subjects give to their productions is geometrical, as in the case of Nic, this leads to other productions—in Nic's case up to four, which she can name. If, however, meanings are concrete-empirical, these analogies have no boundaries and remain more limited in their mode of operation, since any index of the preceding production can suggest the following one (as in Rez's triangle, which suggests "bow tie" or "ball" or "snowman," etc.). We have yet to explain how this development takes place from the procedures of level I to those associated with exhaustive partitioning. We already saw that, in the case of Jer (the free cutting task), it does not result from the formation of partitive operations: on the contrary, it predates these and may thus contribute to their formation. What has to be determined is exactly what happens between the initial state, where subjects are entirely insensitive to the limitations (which to the observer appear as potential perturbations), and the state where all three limitations are overcome by the sudden appearance of the new possibility of exhaustive partitioning. Between these two states, subjects seem to begin to question themselves. From our analyses of free cutting at level IB, one might formulate these questions as follows: What does one do with the "rest"? What are its significant properties? How should one count the pieces? How are they related to the whole (orange or white square)?, etc. Obviously our young subjects do not formulate them like this, or rather do not formulate them at all: they only experience certain difficulties (the limitations thus become perturbations) and their questioning manifests itself only in finding solutions in action, which amounts to accommodating the cutout schema to objects that up to then could not be assimilated (the "rest"). The source of this new possibility should thus be described as an accommodative activity striving to find its form of actualization, since there is already activity but not yet the proper solution. The solution or new procedure is mediated through the channels of obstacles to overcome and limitations to remove. This shows clearly that new possibilities, at the level of stage transitions, are oriented activities and thus tools in the service of reequilibration rather than stable states of equilibrium, since their actualization goes together with development and each state of equilibrium once attained becomes part of reality. We are touching here upon a property specific to possibility and somewhat paradoxical: to the observer and in retrospect, it appears "possible" to overcome the limitations of level I; but for those at that level, this was not yet possible. Still, once this liberation becomes possible, the new possibility gets actualized and thus makes its entry into reality. Thus, possibility as such is not at all a state but a transition arising from a disequilibrium and characterizing reequilibration as a process, and which transforms into reality once the process is terminated.

Once this is said, it appears that level II—characterized as it is by exhaustive partitioning (without "remainders")—soon attains the status of co-possibilities, because once the square is divided in two by a midline, it can also be divided by another, etc. At this point it seems appropriate to stress the role choice plays in the formation of possibilities and to distinguish two types of choice. When passing from one level to the next, as from level I to level II, there is naturally a series of choices involved in the accommodative activity that we discussed in the preceding section. These choices consist in selections that are "best." On the other hand, successive choices made within a level, such as the generation of new possibilities at level I, proceed (as will be shown in more detail in chapter 11) from the fact that as soon as subjects see one possibility as resulting from a free choice, this is sufficient to bring about the realization that at least one other combination could have been chosen, both of them equivalent to each other: this explains the step-by-step progressions characteristic of level I. On the other hand, the progress characterizing transition to level II and the emergence of partitioning procedures and co-possibilities consists in the fact that the following (equivalent) possibility is no longer discovered after the fact (i.e., after the result of one selection becomes visible) but is anticipated and conceptualized as an analogy at the same time as the preceding one. Thus, the subject Bel, for example, begins with a vertical cut through the square but immediately changes to a horizontal one, just as if he already meant to do this when executing his first cut, the second being envisioned as completely equivalent to the first even though it was not chosen as the initial cut; similar reactions were evident with the choice of the two diagonals. Recall the co-possibilities chosen by subjects of the same age levels in the path situation (chapter 2), where they indicated that between A and B a path may be straight, curved, or zigzag.

However, even though co-possibilities constitute a clear progress in multiplying possibilities, they do not preclude further occasional use of successive analogies, particularly when subjects go on from one family of co-possibilities to another. Thus, as already noted in the sections on bipartitioning and tripartitioning, even though the procedure of exhaustive partitioning facilitates co-possibilities by means of symmetries, the latter tend to produce new pseudonecessities when subjects are asked to produce dichotomies, and even pseudoimpossibilities such as those observed with the instruction to produce three equal parts (as in the case of Fer). Therefore, we had to distinguish two sublevels at level II, one where the symmetries impose these limitations, the other where subjects liberate themselves from them. These two sublevels correspond partly to the two types of co-possibilities already discussed: a *concrete* type, where subjects limit themselves to what they can realize, and the other, which we call *abstract*, where the actual cuttings only represent examples of the many conceivable variations.

To sum up the facts observed about the impact a new possibility has on the discovery of subsequent possibilities, we shall group under the term *transposition* those used at the first level: (1) For example, going from one dichotomy to another using one midline and then the other, or from there to a diagonal or both. (2) Second, we see iterated reproduction, as when subjects cut off a strip, then two, three, etc., up to five, where they stop (Pat, 7;6), or proceed by taking off the contours (one strip at each side) until only a small square is left in the middle (found already with Jer at 5;0 but without awareness of continued possibilities). (3) Then there is a conjunction of two transpositions, when midlines are combined with diagonals into a single plan (Bel, 6;5); or when the square is first cut into two superposed or lateral halves, each half being further divided into three or four parts (Gin, 8;1); or, again, each lateral half (i.e., rectangle) is divided by its own diagonal (Pat at 7;6, who cuts by a midline one of the quarters formed by the two diagonals of the original square). (4) Finally, we find nested partitions when subjects (like Fer at 8;2) divides the square into quarters and each quarter into further small squares, without going beyond.

On the other hand, when subjects give up symmetrical or regular shapes, they attain at last the level of abstract co-possibilities, which are characterized by the idea of a multiplicity of possibilities of which the actual productions are considered to be nothing but examples. Ana (9;0), for example, after having replaced her vertical and oblique, symmetrical strips by simple and double curved lines, adds that she could do "many more," and for a dichotomy she connects two opposite angles of the square by various curves and zigzag lines. Another type of variation consists in dividing the square first into two heterogeneous parts of variable sizes and then furnishing one with small squares or small irregular sections, while leaving the other intact or garnishing it with other shapes (Man, 8;4), etc. These variations can affect a whole series of squares, with transitions projected and carried out continuously from one square to the next. We may further note order changes or decompositions (such as from an inner circle to various curved lines), or again multiple changes of position of a single small element over different regions within the square.

Once the limitations resulting from symmetry requirements are overcome, the subjects pass rapidly beyond the level of a few concrete realizations to follow the course of new procedures and variations with multiple possibilities, indefinite in number, up to the recursive procedures of unlimited iterations characterizing level III.

5

Bipartitions and Duplications

with A. Henriques-Christophides

To complete our analyses of the relations between partitive operations and the procedures that precede and probably prepare them, we decided to compare bipartitions or divisions in halves to their inverse — duplication. Bipartitions have already been discussed in the preceding chapter, but only as a special case of cutting a square into two parts of any size. In this chapter, we will examine divisions into halves of a rectangle of about 10×20 cm, which facilitates the task (hence it will be interesting to find again in the youngest subjects procedures of nonexhaustive subtractions); we will use folding, cutting, and drawing. What is original about this task is that once a sheet has been divided in half (or into "two equal parts," etc. the vocabulary to be adapted to the subjects), the halves will then be presented as such with the instruction to reconstitute the whole. Thus we say to subjects, "I had a sheet of paper, and I've cut it in half [or some other term the subject understands]. Here is one of the halves; the other half is hidden. Can you guess what the paper was like before I cut it?" As usual, after each response, we ask: "Can you do it another way?" etc. Obviously, this division into halves and then relating these again to the whole poses a particular problem for the conception of possibilities, and it is not surprising to find that its solution represents a fairly late acquisition. We do not necessarily always present the same kind of paper — in fact, any type of surface will do, and many different configurations can be used so long as the two parts have equal surface areas, but they do not need to be isomorphic.

Level I

We shall not further insist here on the difficulty of dividing a surface in half experienced by the subjects at this first level, since this was already discussed in chapter 4, where it was explained as resulting from the primacy of *subtraction* over *partition* into equal parts. We find that the youngest subjects do not understand the task of division into halves. Therefore, we have substituted a simpler task, presenting two animals lying down, of which one is shown to be twice as long as the other (we don't insist on the term "twice as long," which young children do not comprehend for quite some time). Since the bigger animal has to eat twice as much as the smaller one, we give to the small one two or three beans, "food," in the form of a small rectangle, a triangle, and a long rectangle, asking the child to imagine what the big animal should get:

Cri (5;5), for one bean to the small animal (S) gives two to the big one (B); for two to S, she gives three to B; for three to S she gives four to B; thus, each time $n+1$, with no doubling. "Would it be fair to give B six [for three to S]?" *Yes, because he's bigger.* We give a small rectangle to S. She first gives an identical one to B, then replaces it by one that is slightly bigger. The same reactions with a small triangle to S, as well as with the long rectangles and finally a square, with no size relationships between the items for S and for B.

Jea (5;6) displays the same additive reactions for the beans: $1 \rightarrow 2$, $2 \rightarrow 3$, etc. With the small rectangle, we ask him to give "a bigger one, twice as big, because your cat is twice as big as mine." He only gives a rectangle a bit larger, but not nearly twice as large. Same reactions with the triangle. With a long rectangle he seems to understand, adding to that for S another, identical one for B (thus reaching for a moment the subsequent level); but the square he places on a sheet of paper, cutting around it the perimeter of a rectangle only slighter larger than the square.

May (6;7) initially displays the same additive reactions, including for the rectangles and the triangles. We then ask him to give a cookie three times as big as mine: big and once again as big as mine. This time he puts two the same size together, which seems to be a duplication but is understood as $1+1$, as formulated in the request. The proof is that with the square he simply makes it slightly larger for B.

At level IB, subjects start out as at IA by simple additions, occasionally composing two exemplars of the small items but only with the rectangles; they fail with the triangles (with arbitrary enlargements), and even with the squares (e.g., Mic at 6;3). It is only at 7;1 (Tot) that subjects go on (but still with $2 \rightarrow 3$ and $3 \rightarrow 4$ for the beans) to formulations such as: *I do the same thing two times. I know: it is twice as big.* This realization leads directly to level II.

In a word, even with this simplified method, subjects fail to produce doublings at this level. Because they do not comprehend multiplication, they are subject to a pseudonecessity that limits their notion of *greater than* to only an additive procedure.

Level IIA

At level IIA, division in half no longer presents any problem and passes imperceptibly from symmetries to varied sectionings, always conserving the equality of the two halves. However, with doubling, we certainly find important advances in that subjects now definitely comprehend the task and attempt to find the total area, of which the visible part represents one half; but at level IIA, subjects still fail to produce equal surfaces or produce only approximations:

Phi (7;7) begins with divisions along the midlines and the diagonals, then divides into fourths and distributes these, saying, *There are two too many*, even hiding them in his hand. It takes him long to understand that in this case the halves are those of the first division, even though subdivisions were performed later on each of the two halves. As for doubling ("Guess what the other half was like before I cut it"), he begins with a good approximation (in length); but when asked: "Could it be some other way?" he draws it much too large. "Is that not too big?" *I think it was a long one.* "You think so?" *Was it a square?* He does have before his eyes the half cut out by the experimenter.

Suz (7;1) only produces halves by medians and diagonals and only proceeds by folding (although we suggested that she could also use cutting or drawing). For the doubling task, we present a fairly large rectangle for her to reproduce on a sheet of paper: she imagines the other half in the form of a large half-circle. We present a smaller rectangle: this time she draws an entire circle, smaller than the semicircle before, but more than twice as large as the rectangle. Then she invents the useful method of applying the small rectangle against the paper from which she will take the half to be found: this helps in creating parts on the same scale as the original, but with different shapes—triangles and various trapezoids. We suggest a semicircle, which she finds "too large" compared with the given half; then another, which she finds "too small"; and, finally, a small circle, which she accepts as equivalent.

Kat (8;5) begins as usual, then divides into halves along an oblique close to a median. But in the doubling task, she shows a sheet much too large; even when we tell her that the other half was the same size as the one she has, she divides the large sheet in two, draws on one of the halves the "half" to be presented, and gives as its complement (thus, the other half to be constructed) not a surface equal to it but half of the large sheet itself, justifying her choice by saying: *I've cut right in the middle*, which essentially means *I've made a half, too*. After another explanation, she finally offers a symmetrical shape, although with irregular items.

Isa (8;3) produces halves not only with oblique but also with zigzag and curved lines, taking care to produce two equal parts. In doubling she shows progress, giving complementary parts of about equal dimensions and in different positions. But, when given a quarter of a circle, she no longer respects this requirement and offers a square and then a rectangle as complements—as if the task was to find not another half, but rather a form from which the quarter circle was taken.

Added to the incomprehension of the problem at level I, these reactions of level IIA clearly show that the reconstruction of a whole from its parts is much more difficult than division of a whole into two halves, even when the forms are similar. In fact, subjects who can accomplish exhaustive bipartitions and who have thus reached a level beyond what was called in the previous chapter *subtractions* (except for a momentary slip in the case of Phi, because of a failure to establish a hierarchy between successive dichotomies) still reason as if the half presented had been obtained by simple subtraction (see in particular Isa) and their task simply to produce an analogous piece. Or again they attempt, as in chapter 3, to imagine the hidden part of an object of which only a fraction is perceptible; but that amounts to the same, since the visible part results only from having been taken out of a larger unit (by subtraction). Although the symmetry between the visible and the invisible parts was immediately recognized in chapter 3 even by subjects at level I, in the present situation it is only at level IIB that subjects arrive at this conclusion. The reason is that in chapter 3, the whole was still present in some way, even though partly hidden; whereas in the present situation the whole does not exist any more as such, having been cut up by the experimenter.

The basic difficulty, which constitutes the originality of the present experimental situation, is, thus, that the problem does not require the construction of possibilities oriented toward concrete realizations to be implemented (as is the case for the division in half), but requires retroactive inferences or reconstructions of possibilities already realized before the task. In other words, the possibility in question is what the experimenter *might have done* to obtain her half and not what the subject *can do* to divide a surface in half. All that we know about the way children come to develop conscious awareness indicates that it is always at first directed toward a goal and the result of actions instead of toward preceding states: a fortiori, it must be the case that a possibility in the past, a historical one, or one to be attributed to another's acts, requires more complex inferences than a finalized one, which concerns the choice of procedures oriented toward a result to be obtained. In fact, the problem subjects have to solve is not a simple division in half, which is easily solved at this level, nor a simple doubling, which is no more difficult than division in half, in real action; rather, it requires a composition of the doubling the subject has to perform to reconstruct the original surface and the division in half, which subjects must attribute to the experimenter in order to interpret correctly the shape and the surface of the half presented to them. Thus, it is to be expected that subjects will generally react at a lower level in this task than they did in the first part of the interview, since the reconstruction of past possibilities requires such compositions of reciprocal actions.

Levels IIB and III

When observing children 8–9 years of age, we see middle sections other than symmetrical ones, and the problem of duplication is essentially solved:

Lau (7;6, advanced) divides into symmetrical halves or produces oblique sections; but for the latter, he always checks the equality of the parts constructed by superpositioning. Most probably because of this methodical way of proceeding, he succeeds in solving the problem of duplication: for a small rectangle he immediately draws its double right on top of the model, then does the same with a transverse cut, turning the whole construction by 45 degrees. "Do you think this is different?" *Yes, because it's placed differently. There is still another* [a diagonal the other way]. We present a quarter of a circle: he immediately completes it to a semicircle.

Ala (9;2) proceeds first by vertical parallels, saying: *I'll give six pieces to you and six to me or eight to you and eight to me.* She then draws correctly the diagonals of the two halves of the rectangle and correctly divides the resulting part. Then she draws a large triangle, with its top touching the middle of the upper side of the horizontally oriented rectangle and its base parallel to the lower side of the rectangle before her: she checks to see whether the other triangles have the same surface. *This corner joins that corner: this is for you, that is for me.* Then she partitions the central triangle and the strip at the base, etc. As for the duplications, she proceeds by symmetries, placing similar parts side by side or in L or T shapes to represent possible initial totals.

Sid (9;3) displayed the same reactions for division into halves, except that the angles inside the rectangle introduce symmetries and equivalences so that the equality of the halves becomes apparent. The same combinations as Ala's are produced for duplications.

Mur (10;10) stays with the simplest types of halving, by midlines and oblique lines, and with simple copying for duplication, before putting the halves together in different ways.

Phi (10;10) generates multiple halvings by means of angular and zigzag shapes, but he does not think that there are very many possibilities. To duplicate rectangular forms, he gives the usual combinations; with the quarter circle, however, he first gives two unequal pieces, which he then equalizes and puts together in various ways. He estimates the total number of possibilities as around *four or eight.* "No more?" *I don't think so.*

Nan (11;5) adds to the usual halvings a rectangle inside the large one, saying, *With cross-ruled paper, if I count right* [the squares of the central rectangle and of the borders], *I could do it like that.* In duplication, she puts rectangular halves together in various ways: "Still others?" *Many. I can turn the two around all sorts of ways.* "How many? Ten, 100, 1,000?" *Ten, I think.*

Fre (10,5) performs multiple divisions, varying oblique cuts, and adds: *I could go on like that, make more and more like that.* "How many lines?" *One hundred, no more.* In the duplication task, he is the first one to realize that the small rectangle we present him with is not necessarily half of a figure of the same shape but could have come from a trapezoid consisting of this rectangle A and two triangles B and C such that $B+C=A$.

It can be seen that, aside from Lau, subjects do not comprehend duplication before the age of 9–10 years. And even Lau, who succeeds for reasons already indicated, only has a rudimentary concept of part-whole relations: he considers a whole figure containing a transverse section as different when slightly inclined, as though its position in the plane could change its internal structure.* From the initial recognition that the presented half is part of a whole and that the other half must have the same surface, there are still a number of advances to be made. Lau, for instance, believes that the two halves are necessarily adjacent to each other and that the whole must be of the same shape as the halves; whereas Ala and the others that follow know that the two halves may come from a whole of a totally different form (such as L, T, etc.), even though they still produce only halves identical in shape to the stimulus. The next step is in the same general direction toward increasing relativization, as when subjects begin to understand that the half to be reconstructed may also have a different shape from the one presented: this is the case of Fre, who considers this half as possibly having been cut off from a trapezoid. Finally, the number of possibilities considered is also part of relativization, since if subjects are able to see the different forms as part of a recursive system of intrinsic variations, then the number of possibilities is unlimited. Fre (the most advanced of these subjects) is not far from such a concept when he says, "I could go on like that." But his estimate remains rather conservative when he then specifies: "One hundred, no more." Phi and Nan are still more conservative: 4, 8, or 10 possibilities in all.

At level III, abstract co-possibilities such as Fre's (i.e., a greater number of possibilities than those given as examples, but still limited in number) become indeterminate in intension and unlimited in extension:

Dav (9;10) is intermediate between levels IIB and III. Having found that two halves can be obtained by zigzag or sinusoidal cuts, he adds: *I could go on like that for a long time, as long as you want, in both directions* [lengthwise and across], *I could make a whole bunch of strange shapes.* The expression *as long as you want* is a good translation of "unlimited," but *a bunch of* is still more restricted, which becomes obvious when he tries out divisions with differently shaped halves: *That's harder. It has to be the same size.* "You could continue for a long time?" *Not with these: this is harder.*

Pat (10;7) accomplishes the progress of giving laws of transformation. In duplicating, he applies lengthwise the half he constructed against the model and begins to move his half by a very small amount—first up, then down: *There are 1,000 possibilities, even more.* Then he repeats the procedure transversely: *Again, there are 1,000 like that.* "Can you explain?" He marks a series of points on the immobile side. "I don't understand." *You make a point, then the line, and you start over again a little farther.* "And you are able to count them?" *No, you*

---

*Recall that for young children a square turned on its corners is no longer a square.

can't. . . . It's infinite. After that, he makes one half rotate about an angle of the other: *You can still have a thousand, it's also infinite. . . . That could be anything. I could come up with infinitely many ideas to do no matter what.* "With any kind of half?" *Yes.* "And with any whole, one can have an infinity of halves?" *No* [not having thought out all the different possible forms halves may take]. . . .

Yve (11;4), for dividing in half: *There are infinitely many ways,* including the ones *that do not work* [unequal dichotomies]. To put similar halves together, *There are all kinds of possibilities.* "How many?" *Ten thousand. Even more.* "You could count them?" *That would require enormous amounts of patience.* As for nonconvergent but equal halves, *One can make all possible shapes.*

This progress illustrates the two characteristics of higher ranking co-possibilities: the indeterminate intension (seen in Yve) and the unlimited extension. When a recursive law is hinted at, for example, Pat refers to a continuum of points, giving a fine instance of intrinsic variation.

6

Free Construction with Hinged Rods

with A. Blanchet and D. Leiser

The first three chapters of this book treat children's free combinations, spontaneously conceived toward a goal so general that it is always attained (possible positions of three dice on a cardboard, possible paths between two points in a plane, etc.). Other studies (chapters 7–10) concern possible solutions to a problem posed by the experimenter that cannot be solved immediately (raising a water level, etc.). In the present task, we study free combinations without a problem but where there are constraints resulting from a complex material. Thus the only problems subjects have to deal with are learning how to use the material and to imagine the various compositions that can be realized. In a situation like this, certain goals or idealizations may naturally occur; they are in no way imposed, however, but only proposed by the children themselves (whether they wish to make a "square" or even a "tiger"): the meaning or content of the constructions is thus secondary. What is of interest here are the procedural possibilities – that is, the developmental advances noted in the methods of construction themselves.

The material consists of 30 rods, 12 cm long and 8 mm thick (square sections), plus 8 small bars of the same width but only 7–8 cm long. In addition, we present children with 20 identical metal joints made of two grooved parts in which one can insert the end of a rod on either side. The joints are adjustable so that different directions can be given to the rods: the two rods can either be placed as extensions of each other — —; parallel ||; at a right angle ⌐; or at any angle whatsoever (on a plane or vertically). We simply ask subjects, "What can you make with this?" For the youngest children only, we demonstrate how the rods can be inserted in the joints. If after some exploration of the material a subject only produces very simple and isolated connections, we ask if he or she could "build some constructions," which does not impose any particular goal but incites subjects to imagine more complex connections. After each production, we pursue our usual questioning ("Could you do something different?", etc.) but without making any suggestions, except for showing sometimes how three rods can be joined to build a trihedral angle and seeing what subjects can do about models in three dimensions.

The specific character of this study consists thus in examining two kinds of possibilities as they become more and more closely related, possibilities that derive from different sources. One kind is that offered by the material, which subjects have to discover through more or less crude or directed explorations. These are experiential in nature: as *physical possibilities*, they can be compared to the potential outputs compatible with the connections of a mechanical system, but subjects can only learn about them by trying out for themselves all the different connections. The other kind are the capacities subjects themselves can acquire by their actions, utilizing the physical possibilities offered but going beyond simple connections by imagining higher order combinations, which may or may not involve specific goals and standards of optimal performance or improvement. The possibilities inherent in subjects' actions or capacities are of the same kind as those discussed in the preceding chapters (the possible paths of chapter 2, the possible partitions of chapter 4, etc.); but in the present case, subjects also utilize material instruments having properties related to a set of physical possibilities, which need to be known beforehand or to be discovered in the course of construction: we speak in this case of *instrumental possibilities*. Briefly, physical possibility has to do with possible effects of a particular modification of the material (a particular juncture and its effect on the stability of the construction), whereas instrumental possibilities concern the actions to be performed and coordinated to obtain the constructions chosen. Whereas the former concerns the causalities that determine any compositions whatever, the latter (a special case of procedural possibility) subordinate these to goals.

Level I

The subjects of level IA stay with physical possibilities, which they discover by trial without any definite plans. Each trial constitutes a kind of project in that subjects attempt to find out if such and such a connection is feasible, which amounts to considering it possible, but they accept it as such only after it is has been actualized. Such projects thus generate hypothetical possibilities that lead to failures or successes, with one possibility engendering the next in analogical succession:

Car (5;0) begins by aligning all the joints, leaving them more or less open. She calls this *a serpent* (after the fact). Then she inserts two rods into the two ends of a joint in parallel fashion ($\boxminus$). After that, she arranges them like this: $\wedge$ with a juncture at the top, then two rods side by side and a third extending from the second. Then a right angle $\ulcorner$ followed by $\vdash$. She attempts an upright construction, which does not stand up; she returns to her linear and parallel horizontal patterns, which she continues up to 6 rods, then 10, to the last of which she connects 2 more in oblique fashion. She goes on in this way without stopping, undoing them and starting over and over again. At last she produces a Z and two wider angles.

Val (5;6) also begins by putting only joints together, but with spaces between them. When informed about the possibility of inserting the rods, he links two in parallel. After that he varies the angles, and, delighted by this discovery, he produces a great number of these constructions, either pulling them close together in complete disorder or arranging them around a square that he was able to build. Having accidentally rotated a hinge by 180 degrees, he succeeds in having three pairs of rods in vertical position. Since, in the beginning, he had announced: *I'll say what it is when I've finished*, he now discovers that it is an *airplane*. A jumble of right angles and others becomes *a garage*. His explanations are easier to follow when he calls a T a hammer, extending its handle by three rods.

Ari (4;1) begins with a square that's not quite closed, then pulls the rods close together in parallel; one of the joints thus liberated she uses for a vertical bar. A 10 degree bend in another joint gives her the idea of putting a second hinge in the same corner. She succeeds in building an enclosure with two levels, covering it with rods laid side by side without joints. But even now she sticks to her cautious behavior of *I tell you after*. "Is that a house?" *I tell you when it's all done*.

Compared with other, more usual kinds of free constructions, this task shows that these young subjects, when confronted with unknown material where they have to discover the connections that can be made, do not directly think of possibilities. They act as though they believe that any schema whatsoever can be adapted to any object whatsoever: somewhat awed by the resistance offered by the material and not yet able to correct themselves after a bad move, they seem to doubt that accommodation is possible (like children at the sensorimotor level when confronted with an entirely unfamiliar toy). The subjects are thus placed in a position where they have to distinguish what the material permits (i.e., physical possibility) from what they can expect to be able to accomplish by their own actions; in this situation, their attempts derive from an elementary form of possibility *in statu nascendi*, which can be expressed as: "It is possible (if I act in such and such a way) that this would be possible (in the sense of physically feasible)." This explains the series of pure trials and errors that we observed; there is, to be sure, analogical reapplication of certain successful schemes, but not as yet any sign of self-correction or readjustments. This also undoubtedly explains the curious cautions expressed by a number of subjects, who refuse to indicate their goal even in the course of construction: "I'll say what it is when I've finished" (Val) or "I tell you after" (Ari).*

---

*B. Inhelder and her group have frequently observed this type of conduct at this age: it is thus not exceptional or accidental.

Thus, level IB is characterized by two new developments: the ability and desire for self-correction and the subjects' willingness to announce what they intend to build right from the beginning. We are, thus, dealing here with the emergence or extension of instrumental possibilities.

Kat (5;6), who announces that she is going to make a house, arranges the rods into a square after having corrected the direction of a hinge that was oriented the wrong way. She extends this quadrangle by two elements designed to represent the second floor, but she has difficulty orienting those that represent the entire construction. After a few corrections, she succeeds (the structure is two-dimensional). Then she proposes to make a flower, a diamond on a stem. This necessitates correcting two of the initial angles. She adds two oblique elements for "leaves." Since all her constructions are on a horizontal plane, we suggest that she build a flagpole that can stand up. She first aligns two sticks and, keeping these in her hand, makes a stand out of two others. Then she tries for a long time to put a joint in: *It's that thing that won't work.* She adds two more sticks linked to the others: *That stands up even less well.*

Cor (5;6) represents a good example of perseverance in applying corrections to get a roof on top of a church and then a hat on a man—everything within a two-dimensional design; however, she tries to put in connections instead of simply juxtaposing the sticks; attempting to insert a second joint within the 90 degree angle of a hinge and to place a cross into that angle. Then she says, *I've got a better idea*, and inserts into one of the roof joints a vertical rod with a joint at its top with a 45 degree angle, into which she inserts an oblique bar that is oriented the wrong way (downward instead of upward). She corrects the error, commenting: *Perhaps by putting it like this* [correct orientations, but with simple superpositions]. *No, that wouldn't hold.* At last: *I have a better idea. This time I've thought it out in my head*, and she rebuilds the whole square, redirectioning the joints until successful completion. To make a rod stay in vertical position like a flagpole, she simply fits it into a joint at the base (two juxtaposed parts). It falls, so she adjoins a shorter rod: *It takes a small one to tie it.* The structure collapses again and she pulls the rods farther apart. When this fails, she modifies the distance between the rods until relatively successful completion: *This works.*

Gil (6;8): To keep a rod in upright position, he fits it to a joint and places this construction on a horizontal bar. To correct this after it falls, he surrounds the base with more rods.

Jos (6;11) begins by fitting a vertical joint to the base of the rod to be kept in upright position: "Can you make it more solid?" He adds another rod on top, and after this does not work he adds to the base another joint right next to the first. *Legs. People can stand up because they have legs.* As this still does not work, he somewhat absurdly tries to install a base joint at a 90 degree angle with only one end resting on the floor. After that, he connects two vertical rods by means of a joint; to make it more solid, he adds a joint at one-third, another at two-thirds of the height of one of the rods (without linking the two rods). But this senseless maneuver gives him the clever idea to turn the exterior ends of these joints toward the ground and to insert rods to buttress the construction.

The progress evident in these reactions (relative to those of level IA) is that subjects, convinced that success is possible, conceive plans and announce them openly. They do not relinquish their efforts, at least not immediately, in case of failure; rather, they try to correct their constructions and to improve their actions. However, one drawback of these positive aspects is the way in which confidence in their capacities leads subjects to try anything, coming up with absurd modifications as well as adequate corrections. When Jos attempts to construct his flagpole by supporting it with only one-half of a joint, or when he installs hinges at different heights on only one of the two, it would be difficult for him to find a justification for these ideas, and yet the latter idea made him discover the ingenious solution of buttressing the construction. Trying anything to see what it does, subjects essentially remain at a level of empirical, extrinsic variations; however, some of their successful corrections provide them with a beginning of more intrinsic understanding.

Level II

From this level on, even the level IIA subjects attempt tridimensional constructions. But aside from a few successful, additive constructions (such as building piles, etc.), only at level IIB do we find more generalized coordination. Here are some examples of level IIA:

Mar (6;11) proposes to build a house, beginning with a well-constructed square of which he then constructs a replica. "How is this going to be?" *Like this, like this*, [he indicates the levels]. A badly placed joint is immediately corrected. Once the levels are superposed he covers them with a flat roof, but because he prefers a slanted roof he quickly constructs a triangle, which is also well put together (with a joint at the peak at a 60 degree angle). Three triangles thus constructed are simply placed on top of an empty cube, connected by a bar without joints at their peaks. Everything collapses, but he successfully corrects it by using two bars joined together. He tries to build a flagpole on a single joint, then on two; *No, this will never work*. He puts up two horizontal bars, one opposite the other, which makes the rod fall to the side. He sees that he needs two more across, but he places them at one-third of the total height, achieving a half victory: *It does not fall down all the way!*

Los (7;5) constructs something in *the shape of a tent*, but *that does not stay straight*; then a well-articulated triangle and a similar rectangle. After that, he goes on to three dimensions, the rods piled up (without joints) in the form of a cube and *a garage* with three vertical walls. For the flagpole he uses a slanted buttress, and when this turns out to be insufficient he stabilizes it with closely spaced bars aligned on the flat surface. He then sees that this system is sufficient without buttresses to keep the flagpole upright.

Van (7;8) soon constructs cubic piles, superposing rods without joints; she also builds well-articulated constructions on the plane (diamonds, etc.). We show her, to see what she would make of it, a trihedral structure made of two horizontal bars joined together at an angle of 90 degrees and a vertical bar elevated over this juncture (which means that this rod goes through two joints): *Oh, yes, how did you do that?* "What could you do with that?" *Squares like that.* She indicates with gestures a cube, of which she then constructs the base out of three rods placed to form three of the four angles, with others simply piled on top. "How can this be made to hold?" *Oh, I understand: you've strung two together!* She uses the trihedral structure, transposes the double joint on another angle, and finally ends up with a cube, which is slightly flawed in that one of its vertical ridges consists of two juxtaposed ascendants rather than a simple rod: *I don't know what I did, there is a gap* [between the two bars]; *it's not like the others. . . . There are two here!*

Ant (7;2), to make the flagpole stand up, puts it between two bars placed opposite each other: it falls to the side, then he has the correct idea of adding a bar across, first at the base then near the end of one of the initial bars. But to do this he makes the flagpole lie down horizontally as if confusing planes and directions. He had, however, indicated his plan correctly with gestures: "Show me how you would like to put the bar." *Like that* [again the correct gestural indications]. Nevertheless, he repeats the same procedure as before.

Ced (8;6) constructs *a tunnel* with three rods ⊓ , which collapses despite the joints placed at the two bases; he adds two rods on the flat surface to the right: another failure. He adds to each one another rod and puts six symmetrically to the left, which makes the structure stable. He then tries to build a table but does not succeed in keeping the crossbars in upright position. He finally decides to continue building the piles.

In reading these protocols, one can see that the instrumental possibilities get actualized on the level of the plane (the well-articulated squares and triangles of Mar, Van's diamonds, etc.), and the same is true for the vertical flagpole in some cases (Los). Likewise, constructions in three dimensions are built successfully so long as they are simple additive stacks, since in all these cases the physical possibilities remain simple and well understood, facilitating action. On the other hand, three-dimensional compositions fail, not because of a lack of imagination in the projects, nor because volume entails a greater number of relationships than a plane, but because the physical possibilities imply more complex coordinations and articulations (as in Van's "Oh, you've strung two together," when commenting on the position of the joints) and because the subjects have not taken the precaution of exploring these particular forms of physical possibilities before going ahead with the instrumental possibilities. Now, it is striking that at level

IIB subjects begin to explore more completely these possibilities, as if they had just passed through level IIA and, made cautious by the failures, knew that they would have to go back to analyze the physical possibilities. More simply, being more advanced in their development of causal concepts, they suspect that before projecting any instrumental possibilities it is necessary to begin by determining in detail the various physical possibilities and to understand them:

Vil (9;1) begins to make elementary linear and parallel connections, taking the joint off: "What are you trying to do?" *I'd like to see what I can do.* After that he makes various angles and, finally, a well-structured square. We show him a trihedral structure: *This gives me an idea.* He then succeeds in building a cube, after having reconstructed the triped with difficulty in terms of directing the hinges and finally understanding their junction. He indicates the possibility of adding another, similar level.

Col (9;7) similarly begins with simple linear and angular junctions and then constructs a square. After that, he adjust two vertical rods on two horizontal ones and then covers these with a perpendicular girder. The structure seems fragile, so he moves the hinges toward the center and slants the vertical rods, adding two others. A bar placed lengthwise along the base consolidates the construction. We propose the trihedral and he reconstructs it, completing it with a symmetrical replica to finish with the base of a cube. Again, he adds a level instead of closing it.

Ris (9;6), after a few preliminary linear and angular attempts, builds two triangles connected by their peaks, but these remain unstable. Similarly, she builds two squares connected by two transverse bars at their upper ends and adds two bars near the base for consolidation, but she experiences some difficulty in positioning the hinges. She finally succeeds in constructing a stable cube, which she converts into a chair by adding a back.

Jan (10;10), after some very simple manipulations, proposes no less than to build a tiger: the body is a prism and the head a kind of an *M*, but inclined forward.

Two interrelated characteristics distinguishing this from the preceding level come out quite clearly. The first is a much more intense exploration of the physical possibilities, which we see in the many simple, preliminary attempts that gradually become more complex. The most striking feature of this exploration, however, is the subject's need to understand and not simply be successful. When confronted with the trihedral, subjects do not immediately embark on an analogous project of their own; rather, even in saying like Vil, "This gives me an idea," they first try to rebuild the same construction so as to comprehend the way the hinges work: this explains their success in constructing the cube and other forms. The second characteristic of the constructions (and the reason for their success) is their becoming multiplicative in the sense of coordinated modification of various components—for example, changing the orientation of the hinge at the same time as its location on the bars or the direction of the bars. By contrast, the compositions at level IIA remain additive in the sense of a simple accumulation of adjunctions – for example, the piles produced by almost all of the subjects, the modifications in the base, which are additive accumulations of homogeneous elements. Recall the surprising behavior of Ant, who, after having added horizontal bars to consolidate the base of his flagpole, ends up laying the pole down too as if the aim had not been (even though indicated twice by his own gestures) to make it stand upright.

Level III

Subjects 11–12 years of age present a peculiar situation, which is particular to this study. That situation, we believe, is a consequence of the dual nature of possibilities: physical and instrumental. Thus, rather than showing common or comparable behaviors, these subjects divide into two rather different groups. One manifests progress in continuity with that observed at level IIB in their projects and instrumental realizations, whereas the other focuses on minute, continuous, and quasi-recursive variations, which need to be considered separately. Here are some examples from the first group, which presents no particular problems:

Dav (11;3) restricts himself to two preliminary attempts, a straight line and a 90 degree angle: *I take a look at how that works.* Then he proceeds to build a kind of vertical cross $+$, which he puts up on a horizontal bar that in turn is kept in place by other bars perpendicular to it, also on the flat surface, but each equipped with a vertical construction in the shape of a $\dashv$ and $\vdash$. Of course, he encounters a few difficulties, which he overcomes by correcting them one after the other. He then makes a square, which he completes correctly as a cube, without having to be presented with the trihedral as was done at level IIB.

Syl (12;9) begins in a plane, but adds: *I try to make something not too easy.* She proceeds to do vertical rods, with a constant concern for accuracy: *I don't always see right away which way I turn the hinge, which side it bends so it comes out the way I want it to.* For a cube: *You can't make a diagonal with that. . . . You can't put a joint to the other rod,* and she shows that this is impossible *because of the square at the joint* [she indicates the impossible position]. After the cube she constructs a prism.

Arc (13;10) goes from a square to a pentagon, then to constructions with six vertical branches united at the top so that they make a kind of a star, which he succeeds in closing after some difficulties.

These instrumental successes are dependent on the subject's comprehension of the connections used, a fact already noted when we compared levels IIA and IIB. The subjects of the second group, however, seem to have quite different orientations and aims. Instead of proposing a variety of difficult goals, they aim for the simplest variations and those with the easiest connections, as if the purpose of the game were to discover the elementary transformations of the material (the "too easy" that Syl wants to avoid), even at the risk of appearing somewhat behind; yet there are too many subjects of this kind to consider them as such.

Isa (11;0) takes two hours to describe such continuous variations: she begins with straight lines, then offers three kinds of joined parallels, then various angles pointed upward or downward, then a right angle. From the angles she proceeds to the diamond, the square, and then to a polygon. She joins two parallels in the middle to build on it, which leads to other letter shapes. The angles are then combined to form a pyramid composed of 3, then 6, and finally 10 angular parts; these she replaces with shapes of a house or goes back to her angles to make a star with four and then five corners (with errors and corrections at the junctures). After that she aligns vertical rods on a single base, varying their number. Toward the end only, she returns to three-dimensional constructions, which she compares to a level passage, showing how to install the hinges to obtain perpendicular relations.

Cla (11;2) displays the same reactions with angles and pyramids, then with a series of parallels linked pairwise by means of right angles, the junctions alternating between left and right.

Jos (10;7) builds many parallels oriented horizontally and vertically, arranged like this: ‿ ‾‿ ‾‿ , then some zigzags before getting around to the angles by way of a Z.

These manipulations might be taken for the beginnings of the type of simple exploration found at level IIB if they were of shorter duration. But their duration seems to lend a certain finality to these peculiar behaviors. If this interpretation is correct, these behaviors could be seen as attempts to minimize the role of one's own actions (instrumental possibility) and to maximize the minute variations of physical possibilities inherent in the material. Certainly, these subjects function at a lower level than those of the first group. But up to the final stage there remains a duality between physical and instrumental possibility, in spite of the fact that the former group performs a perfect synthesis of the two as they add to their comprehension of the physical connections imaginative plans that can be actualized.

In chapter 7, we shall return to a discussion of the nature of physical possibility. At this point, it is sufficient to describe briefly the progressive coordination between physical and instrumental possibility. At level I, subjects focus either on the former (IA) or the latter (IB) of the two. At level II, there is progress in coordination: coordination is still imperfect at level IIA, whereas there is mutual facilitation between the two at level IIB, which may be still only local or already quite general. In the first group of level III, there is synthesis with comprehension of both aspects, whereas subjects of the second group focus their instrumental capacities on a more detailed analysis of the variations in physical possibilities.

7

Raising Water Levels

with C. Brulhart and G. Tissot

In chapter 6, we saw that a distinction must be made between physical possibility, having to do with the effects (of a causal nature) that modifications in a complex material can produce; and instrumental possibility (a special case of procedural possibility), which makes use of physical possibilities to build free constructions. In this chapter, we no longer look at free combinations; rather, the subject's freedom is subordinated to a goal, which is to raise the water level of an aquarium by immersing in it a variety of objects. However, since these objects vary a great deal along various dimensions as well as in weight, our analysis will be focused on physical possibility. This type of possibility raises an important epistemological issue: Is the possibility to be seen as residing in the subject, or are all variations and relations—in particular the ones that become translated into laws—nothing but "realities," and what we see as physical "possibilities" (including "virtual effects") only the product of the physical scientist's subjective anticipations and deductions? In particular, the status of *models* of causal explanation, constructed by scientists to give scientific laws their necessary or probabilistic characteristics, is related to this issue. Perhaps the psychogenetic analysis of the beginnings of physical possibility is relevant to the solution of this problem.

The material consists of a cylindrical aquarium into which the child may put a piece of wood, a beaker, a candle, three lead weights, a sponge, a jam jar with a top, a tubular box made of metal, a stone, and an inflatable balloon. We simply ask subjects to use these objects to make the water level rise as high as possible.

Level I

As we have frequently observed in earlier work, the initial behaviors designed to produce a causal effect do not differentiate the objective processes leading to that effect from the subject's actions, which temporarily modify reality but are believed to produce permanently the desired result:

Val (4;11) places into the water two weights, then a sponge, which she tries to keep down at the bottom with her hand. *It's always coming up.* She adds a big weight and a stone. *The water didn't go higher.* She takes the jar without its cover and the piece of wood. *Ah, this time the water went higher.* After this, she announces: *I'll do it over to make the water go even higher.* She takes all the objects out, empties them, and puts them back *underwater.* "Is it the same as before or is it different?" *It's different.* "Why?" *I don't know.* This time she tries to hold down the candle. "Are there some things that make the water go higher than others?" *No, they're the same.*

Isa (4;11) does not bother to keep the lighter objects in the water and to let them float. To make the water rise higher *we need more things*, but one can also just take them out and put them back in, as if this would result in an increase.

Ali (4;9) believes she can raise the water level with just the balloon and agitates the water to make waves: *If one does that* [she now does it with the candle], *that makes it go really high.* Then she puts other objects into the water and concludes that the water has gone up *a little bit* [the piece of wood, the big weight, etc.] or *that makes no difference* (another weight and the stone]. Finally, she discovers that *one can put them all in at once.*

Cor (5;0) takes water with the beaker to fill up the jar, which she then empties into the aquarium. She starts over again using other hollow objects and even tries with the cover of the jar.

Lis (5;5) takes the same beaker, fills it, and pours the water back into the aquarium. "The water went higher?" *Yes.* "Are you sure?" She looks at the water level. *No.* She plunges the tube into the water: *It's going up.* "Do you have another idea?" *I'll let the air out of the balloon, that'll make a wind and make the water go higher.* She tries it. *That does not do anything!* She comes up with the idea that the *stub* [wood] *will make the water go highest, because it's the biggest*, but she does not judge by volume, only comparing the lengths of the wood and the tube: *That will make it go up the same.*

Olg (6;4) still says at her age, *One has to make waves* [which she does with the jar cover]. "Can you make the water go up another way?" *No.* "Try." *I don't know.* "With the wood?" She submerges it. *That way, the water goes up.* "And if you don't submerge it, will it rise?" *No, not at all.* But after a few trials, she comes to attribute the rising of the water level to the size of the objects. From this, she concludes: *We have to put them all in*; but then she predicts that the balloon, even though big, would have no effect, *because it has to be heavy.*

Sca (6;8), on the contrary, holding first various objects (candle, weights, tube) just above the surface as if they should attract the water, then places the deflated balloon over the water, saying, *Perhaps it will pump up the water.* Then, following a series of attempts, he comes to sense the importance of weight; he puts the big weight over the beaker, fills the tube with water, and submerges it, *because the tube that has water in it must be heavy*; he cannot understand why the water level falls.

These observations show, as predicted, a surprising degree of lack of differentiation between one's own action and that which objects exert upon each other. When subjects using their hands submerge objects that would otherwise float, they believe that this can have a lasting effect upon the objects' properties. When Val and Isa want to take everything out and then return the same objects into the aquarium, they act in the belief that by repeating their own action they would produce an objective result. Similarly, Ali and Olg believe that by making waves they can raise the initial water level. The most surprising of the possibilities projected is that of Cor and Lis: take the water out and put it back again, as if this action could increase its quantity. Sca even expects to be able to attract the water by holding the objects over its surface; similarly, Lis, like Sca, wants to have the balloon make a wind to pump up the water. In each case, the physical possibilities are thus seen as resulting from instrumental possibilities, and there is no attempt to look for properly objective causes. Still, in some situations, subjects may temporarily invoke weight or volume, but without systematic exploration or even an adequate reading of the facts observed.

Level II

Starting at 7–8 years of age, physical possibilities come to be treated as autonomous. They are perceived as having characteristics and variations of their own, which the subjects can anticipate and test against the facts to see whether they are physically realizable. This leads subjects of this level to gradually discover the properties of objects. They find ways to keep underwater those objects that would float and thus have less of an effect. The more advanced subjects (level IIB) come to formulate more or less satisfactory explanations based on weight as a factor in submersion and on volume as a factor in the height of the water level. Here are some examples of level IIA, starting with an intermediate case:

Son (7;2) formulates a principle underlying these new reactions: noting that the tube by itself does not stay underwater, she inserts a weight *to see if that makes the water rise*. Here we have an exploration of effects antedating causal interpretations, which does not yet lead to a sufficient explanation: *That should make it heavier* is Son's only comment after that. When she has observed the experimenter raising the water level by submerging the beaker up to its neck (which makes the water rise) and then making it sink by letting it fill up with water, she only notes a global relationship: *It's because the beaker goes down, that makes the water go down, whereas if it's on top, the water goes up again.*

Xav (8;2), on the other hand, after having seen that each weight makes the water rise, holds the candle under one of the weights to keep it submerged, then does the same for all floating objects, using various combinations. But he fails to notice that some of these do not work, such as putting the candle into the jar and closing it. He also cannot understand the different effects resulting from the relative positions of tube and jar, while noting correctly the variations in the water level. When asked if there is a way of knowing how to do better, he takes everything out and starts over again, being aware that he did not bring it up as high as before. The only explanation he finds is that the weights work best *because weights are very heavy*.

Fab (8;8) has similar reactions but makes some additional discoveries, which remain unexplained, however. While exploring for the third time all the objects (taking them out and rearranging them), she notes, *It's always the same, and even a bit lower.* She believes that this is so because of the jar cover, which *remains alone*. She takes the jar, removes the weights, the stone, and the water and closes it with the lid. Then she puts it, empty and closed, into the water: *It rose!* But she so little understands the reason why that she tries to fill it with water: *That would make it rise even higher because that would make it heavier* [she tries]. *It goes down! It rose higher without water!* But she does not know why.

Eva (9;0) puts the tube into the water upright: *I wish this could stand up—that would make it go up higher. . . . The candle won't do it either. . . . If there were weights one could make it go up more, because they're heavy. So that would fill up a bit.* The beaker being in the water, she predicts a change *by putting the stone into the beaker.* [Tries it.] *It didn't go up!* "Do you know why?" *Perhaps because it is heavier, it goes down.* "Is it the weight or the size that makes it rise?" *It's the one that's heavy.* "Size is important?" *Yes, also* [but only by being associated with weight].

And here some cases of level IIB:

Cro (8;8), after several attempts with one object after another: "What is needed to make it rise? *Something heavy.* "Why?" *Because if it's heavy it goes to the bottom and it takes up space, so the water goes up.* To achieve more, he puts a weight into the empty jar, closes it, and makes it sink. *That went up a lot! I'll put in the two other weights and the stone*[which he does]. *Oh! Oh! That went up less than before! I put in too much weight. That's surprising. . . .* He thus does not see that he has in fact reduced volume. He takes out a weight and the stone, which he leaves on the table, but the jar is not closed tightly and fills up with water: *The water went down even more!* The candle in the jar standing up without getting filled surprises him, and he explains this success, saying: *There's something light and something heavy.* The tube half filled, he comments: *It went down! Ah! It is because there is water in there!* He verifies his explanation by emptying the tube, leaving it standing upright: *It went up!* But he forgets that he already attributed a role to the space occupied.

Ste (9;8) also vacillates between weight and volume. He tries to submerge everything. "Would it rise more if it's all underwater?" *I think so.* "Sure?" *I think I'm sure*[!]. "What makes the water rise?" *The weight gain . . . Oh! No, the bigger the contraption, the higher the water level, because it takes up more space.* This gives him the idea of blowing up the balloon: *It goes up*, but he does not generalize to the tube because *it is empty.*

Jea (10;0) soon formulates the hypothesis that raising the water level requires *the most weight underwater.* He puts one object into another *to save some space* so as to use *more objects.* But having compared the weight—*heavier but smaller*—with the candle—*bigger but less heavy*—he concludes that *when it is bigger, that makes it rise higher: it's size* [that is important]. Still, he does not understand why the tube *without water, . . . goes higher*, and only concludes that this contradicts the predominant role of weight, which he had been tempted to revert to again.

Physical possibility exists here in an interaction between objects insofar as these are predicted or inferred by the subjects, who then subject these inferences to selective, empirical tests. This requires that the subject act upon the objects— that is, introduce procedural and even instrumental possibilities, which become actualized in material transformations. These transformations and their results concern physical "reality": they are "possible" only relative to the subject who modifies this reality in action or in thought.

The principal characteristic of level II is thus the continuous interaction between instrumental and physical possibilities, the former manifesting itself in a proliferation of attempts, more unfruitful than successful, and of hypotheses, which are just as likely or more likely to be wrong than right; physical possibilities, however, are gradually discovered, but only through more or less exact interpretation of the observable effects and their confrontation with more or less persistent efforts at causal explanation. In other words, the process begins with the actions of the subject, whose possible variations lead to information and discoveries about the objects and the way they function. These observations act as feedback that suggests new procedures leading to new observations, and so forth.

The two procedures used by subjects that are effective in principle are placing as many objects as possible into the water and keeping them near the bottom and not on the surface by having the heavier objects hold down the floating ones by blocking or cornering them. On the other hand, a number of faulty strategies derive from an erroneous causal interpretation (attributing the rise of the water level to an object's weight), which dominates throughout level IIA and prevents the level IIB subjects from generalizing the role of volume to the jar, the beaker, and the tube (empty or full). Because they attribute the effect to weight, subjects fill empty objects with heavy material to increase their weight ("to make it heavier," as Son said) and not or not only to keep them down. Weight, seen as the expression of a force, may, in some cases, be considered so omnipotent as to pull down the water level (Eva: "Perhaps because it is heavier, it goes down"; and the analogous formulation of Son that "because the beaker goes down, that makes the water go down"). But, in general, weight is seen as pushing the water up, which explains most of the errors in the procedures. At level IIB, the subjects discover the role of volume. Cro thus remarks that weight only makes the object sink so that "it takes up space, so the water goes up"; but this does not prevent him from saying, a bit later, after having made an error: "I've put in too much weight. That's surprising . . . ," without noticing that by putting heavy objects into the closed, empty jar, he has diminished the effective volume. He even maintains that the unexpected success achieved by having the candle hold down the empty beaker is caused by the combination of "something light and something heavy." This shows that even at this level, weight remains an all-purpose concept.

But what is most peculiar about the level IIB responses regarding volume is the subjects' incomprehension of the effect of vessels like tubes when they are filled or empty. In earlier research with A. Henriques, we saw that until 11–12 years of age subjects of level IIB, while beginning to consider volume, still predicted that a table tennis ball with holes would make the water rise more than the same ball without holes because when the holes fill up with water the ball would get heavier and thus have more weight to repel the surrounding liquid.* In fact, the important role of weight can be explained by a difficulty in the estimation of the volume of the displaced water, a difficulty analogous to that encountered in class inclusion: subjects fail to think of the total volume B, the sum of the surrounding water A and the volume A' inside the object, and consider only the action of A' on A. This prevents them from seeing that by emptying the hollow object they set A' to zero and increase A, which becomes identical with B, which means a rise in water level. In short, since they fail to reason about the whole B as composed of $A+A'$, they also fail to understand that if $A'=0$, then $A=B$; or, put more simply, that A increases by the same amount, A', by becoming $A+A'$.

There is nothing unusual about the fact that deductive reasoning should be applied to physical possibilities. It would be easy to show that all the numerous faulty procedures still present at level IIA can be traced to insufficient interpretations of previously observed effects and that the successful solutions derive from inductive or deductive inferences of variable complexity that predict what is physically realizable from what the subject can justify as being possible. Clearly, what is physical in this kind of possibility is only the real or actual, whereas what remains possible can only come from prediction or reconstruc-

*See also J. Piaget and B. Inhelder, *The Child's Construction of Quantities* (London: Routledge & Kegan Paul, 1974).

tion—in other words, it remains relative to subjects' actions. Since these are always subject to factual regulation, they cannot consist simply of free combinations, but only of inferences regulated by facts.

It is informative in this respect to examine the way possibilities are generated at level II. Whereas at level I it proceeds by discontinuous leaps from one attempt to the next, at level II it involves generalizations and quasi-intrinsic variations. We can distinguish at least seven different types: (1) First, a change from manual action to that of an object chosen as a substitute: subjects replace the action of manually holding down an object underwater by that of placing a heavier object on top of a lighter one. (2) Variations in size: having observed the effect on water level of a small weight, subjects add more of these or substitute a bigger one. (3) Variations in number: having seen one weight hold down an object, subjects put several weights together to have them act on it. (4) Change from partial to maximal action: blowing up the balloon after having observed its partial effect. (5) Inversion of an action: the water level having sunk after a wrong move, subjects try the opposite to succeed. (6) Changes in position: placing the piece of wood in vertical position after having observed its effectiveness in a horizontal position. (7) Combination of several factors: "In order for an object to occupy as much place as possible, it has to be both big and under water." Notice the inferential nature of each of these types of processes.

Level III

The two innovations at this level are comprehension of the general role of volume, including that of hollow objects, and the fact that all attempts are directed by deductive hypothetical thinking concerning optimal procedures.

Flo (11;6) succeeds in putting all objects underwater after some difficulties with the balloon. As for the jar, Flo is first surprised that the water level is higher when the jar floats than when it is filled with water at the bottom: *Oh yes, if I put water in there, then there is less water in the aquarium, so the water level is not as high.* We recognize the reasoning described above as being based on the relation $B=A+A'$ or, if $A'=0$), then A increases).

Jos (11;6) already says about the sponge: *That doesn't make the water level rise because it absorbs water.* As for the jar, he empties and closes it, then holds it down with a weight, saying that if the jar were open the water level *would go down because water would be inside.*

Mar (11;10) says about the beaker that when *the water could not get into the beaker, the water went up because the beaker takes up space.* And about the jar: *When it is full, water gets lost: it cannot get out of the jar* [into the aquarium], *so the water level sinks.*

Cat (13;5), after having put a weight into the jar and seen that it had no effect, concludes immediately: *In any case, one cannot say anymore that the more weight there is, the higher the water level.*

Pat (15;4) sums up everything, appealing to *the pressure of volume*. He immediately closes all open objects and then blows up the balloon. All his actions are organized to obtain the greatest possible volume occupied by the objects weighed down to stay underwater.

The evidently deductive nature of this last stage makes it possible to take up once again, but in more general fashion, the problem of the nature of physical possibilities. Minimally, it is easy to show that in no case is this type of possibility accessible without such activities by the subject as deductions, predictions, inferences of various degrees of abstraction, or simply trials, which are hypotheses in concrete acts. Inasmuch as physical possibilities concern aspects that are not as yet actualized, they must necessarily be relative to anticipations of various levels of complexity. On no account can they be identified with a simple recording of facts, since this would be effective only once the expected results were known. But if physical possibilities are not reducible to the reading of observable phenomena, are they then potentially present in objects? The strongest claim that we wish to uphold is that the answer to this question is a definite no. Something in a given state that prepares the following state $n+1$ may be said to be virtual inasfar as it is not observable or not yet observable, but this is still not a possibility; rather, it is a part of reality because it is effective even though not directly observable but only known through inference.

One may object that there are situations where one state n may be followed by several equiprobable states $n+n'$, like a die that can fall on any one of six faces. Yet, once again, an important difference distinguishes what is possible relative to a subject from physical facts: the former exists as a set of synchronous co-possibilities, whereas the latter is only a sequence of events—the die falling on one or the other of its faces. As for equiprobability, to which equipossibility can be reduced, it is measured in terms of frequencies when there is a large number of events. Still, it remains the subject's activity that unites into a simultaneous, conceptual whole what physically exists as a series of independent states. As the adage goes, chance has neither intelligence nor memory, whereas possibilities require both.

8

The Largest Possible Construction from the Same Elements

with E. Ackermann-Valladao and K. Noschis

This chapter, like the following one concerning equidistant relations, treats the formation of possibilities with respect to two activities: the interpretation of goals and the variability in the means to achieve these goals. Whereas progress in the equidistance situation consists in replacing partially erroneous approximations by more precise relationships, the development we shall observe in this chapter—where the children have to attribute meaning to the term *largest possible* (which we take care not to define for them, even if they ask for a definition)—consists in adding the two dimensions that are initially neglected in favor of a single dimension (length or height). On the other hand, the material presented to the child remains the same in terms of number of elements: three small, cubic blocks plus four medium-sized and three large parallelepipeds (the large ones twice as long as the medium-sized ones). As a result, when subjects evaluate *largest possible* in terms of volume, all the different arrangements possible are of equal size, a fact understood by the 11–12 year olds. The problem that concerns us here, given the fairly open character of the task, which subjects may interpret as they wish, is, thus, once again the dynamics of possibilities. These will be examined under two aspects: the multiplication of possibilities by the composition of relationships (and even their overdetermination) and their improvement. In this particular situation, such improvements require compositions between possible relations or variations, because size involves three dimensions. These compositions thus raise the problem of the relations between possibility and necessity, as is, of course, true of all situations where possibilities can be obtained by deductive processes.

Because we wished to allow for the construction of a variety of products, we used blocks made like commercial Lego blocks that lend themselves to various linear and angular concatenations. The initial question is: "Build me the biggest construction you can with this." After that: "Can you make an even bigger thing?" and so on. Somewhat later: "Is there another way to make it even bigger?" And, finally, "What does 'big' mean for you?" and "Can one do it another way?" After each successful construction (i.e., one that holds up), we ask why it is bigger than the preceding one.

Level I

The characteristics seen at this initial level are the limitations and the mode of production as it changes over trials. The former pertain to the goal, which remains unidimensional, and to the means, which, although aimed at improvement, fail to respect the optimalization requirement. The interesting thing about the second characteristic is the phenomenon of *overcomposition* in the multiplication of possibilities; that is, any aspect whatsoever may be related to any other aspect in the course of exploration, without any recognizable order or plan.

Ter (4;5) interprets size as height, building up blocks in stacks of horizontal, superposed layers: a large block (*C*) at the base, a medium-sized block (*B*) on top, another *C*, a *B*, then a *C* supporting two *B* blocks that are aligned and three small blocks (*A*) aligned to form the summit.* This alignment of blocks constitutes an exception to the overall plan, which aims for height. It shows a lack of optimalization that goes unnoticed by the subject. "What did you make?" *They're all on top of each other* [which is precisely not the case for the last five blocks]. "Can one make it bigger still?" *No, they're all on top of each other.* "Really, no bigger?" At this point, Ter has a moment's hesitation; then, instead of trying to correct the construction, he demolishes it and starts anew: two *B*'s superposed at the base, followed by a *B* and an *A* side by side, then one *C* and, again, on top, one *B*+one *A*, aligned. Then a *C* horizontally, and just as he picks up the last *C*, holding it vertically to start, he exclaims joyfully: *Ah!* and places it like that on top of his construction (a nice illustration of an unplanned overcomposition!). He then uses this discovery by holding two *C*'s in his hand over a base; but again two *A*'s+one *B* are aligned horizontally instead of superposed, although he continues to define *the biggest* as *the tallest*.

Eri (5;10) conceives largeness as meaning composed of large blocks only, so he picks the three *C* blocks and places them at 90 degrees to start a square. "What about the others?" *No, it takes only big Legos.* "Isn't it possible to do it another way to build something big?" *Oh, yes* [he assembles three *B*'s with the *A* junctures]. *Like this, it makes a big one* [he closes his square with these *B*+*A* blocks]. "What is it like, your construction?" *Big.* "Why?" *Because the Legos are also big. That one* [a *C*] *is big, that one* [a second *C*] *is big, too, that one* [the third *C*] *too and that one* [three *B*'s] *is bigger—that makes a bigger one than that one and that one.* "Can you do something different that is big?" *I will try*

---

*In the following descriptions, *A* designates the small blocks, *B* the medium-sized ones, and *C* the large ones.

[he assembles the three *C* blocks lengthwise, two *B*'s at an angle, and puts the remaining blocks — two *B*'s and three *A*'s — on top of the row of *C*'s]. *That is bigger than what I did before.* "Why?" *It is longer.*

Dav (5;6) needs to incarnate the concept of bigness in concrete objects. He begins by making a big pistol, piling up seven blocks in three levels. "Can you make the biggest by taking them all?" He assembles two *C* blocks lengthwise; puts three *B*'s on top, one in the middle, and one at each end; then adds the three *A* blocks on top of one *B*. *That's a boat.* "Is it big?" *No, it's only long. . . . Ah, I think I have an idea how to make them bigger.* He aligns all three *C*'s and puts all the other blocks on top. "What is your idea?" *It's a boat that's bigger and longer.* "It can't be made longer?" *No, there are no more pieces* [he does not think of moving *B*+*A*].

Dom (5;6) piles all the blocks up horizontally. "Could it be made bigger?" *Yes.* He undoes his pile and rebuilds it using all the same blocks and in almost identical fashion. *It's taller* [which is illusory]. "Why?" *Because it's bigger.* "Why?" *Because it's taller. The other one was smaller.*

Emi (5;9) begins with a house that is wider than it is high. "Can one make it bigger still?" *Yes.* He takes it apart, leaving only two *C* blocks at the base, which he lines up vertically. he continues building up height but also places some blocks laterally so that the resulting height barely exceeds two *C*'s. "Bigger still?" *No. . . . Yes.* He takes away the two *C* blocks that he had moved to the second level and covers everything with *B* and with *A*. "What about attaching all the Legos?" *Oh! Yes.* He puts up a *C* in vertical position and attaches the remaining *B* and *A* laterally. "Is this house bigger than the first one?" *It's smaller because before I had it "up" and now it's sideways.*

Jos (6;3) connects the three *C* blocks lengthwise with junctures. "Could one make it bigger?" He adds the four *B*'s, making a kind of staircase, which he then extends by placing the steps farther apart.

Niq (6;5) horizontally aligns the three *C* blocks and mounts them with junctures. A second trial is identical, with only the position of the joints changed. On the third trial, however, she adds a *B* lengthwise. Then: *Now I'll make you something tall,* but she succeeds in building only six levels. *It is not as big as the other one* [indicates length with her hands]. *This one is more compact.* She goes back to length and optimalizes by lining up the 10 blocks in a row without a juncture.

Osi (6;11), after a row of three *C*'s+one *B*, suggests when asked to "do it another way": *If you wish, I'll do it by height.* She stacks up three *C*'s+one *B* and attaches one *B* sideways, extending the structure by two-thirds. "Is it bigger or not?" *No, it is smaller* [which is false]. We try to give her a very strong hint: "What if one built something by height and by width?" She does. *I shall make a square. Ah! but that doesn't work. I can only do it by length.*

The first question raised by level I is why we find unidimensional interpretations of size (height or length). It is not likely to be caused by a pseudonecessity in the strict sense. More likely, we are dealing here with an unintentional limitation resulting from the difficulty of coordinating several dimensions. Comparing this with levels II and III, we suggest that there are two ways of composing the relations that characterize the variations in procedures and the interpretations of goals in the formation of new possibilities (many intermediate types of compositions are possible). The more advanced one is what we call *regulated compositions* (for instance, in the logic of relations or in the preoperational functions, etc.). In this case, the variables are selected on an abstract level and coordinated by means of fixed laws of increasing necessity. The other way is without abstraction or rules, and the observables are overdetermined because of their heterogeneity. Subjects tend to establish a heterogeneous variety of relations between these observables, in ever-increasing numbers and types, which change constantly from one action to the next: in these situations, new relations and new compositions are constantly built up. This explains the generative dynamics of possibilities. But these combinations are to regulated compositions what overdetermination is to well-delimited systems: for this reason, we decided to call them *overcompositions*. They can be quite fertile, as in Ter's case, who discovered in the process of picking up a block the possibility of placing it vertically. But they can just as easily lead to erroneous conclusions and interpretations, as when the same child says: "They're all on top of each other," when five blocks are placed side by side on top of the construction.

The mode of composition—facilitating the production of new relationships, but deficient in the regulation of coordinations—thus explains both the procedural flaws and the restriction in interpreting the goals as one dimensional only. What is striking about procedures is not only the absence of optimalization, but also the errors committed in evaluating what is "big" within the subject's own definition of the term: Dom sees as "taller" a stack of blocks that differs from the preceding one only in the relative order of elements (very slightly); Osi considers as "smaller" (in height) a pillar that is in fact slightly taller than the preceding one. Emi labels "smaller" a building that is taller but wider because, in addition to blocks placed on top of others, there are now some "sideways." The absence of optimalization (general except for Niq) is a natural consequence of this: the one-dimensional size concept used by these subjects to aim for either height or length does not yet involve that of a linear interval between two points, but rather a global idea of an envelope, where the positions of the elements embraced by the envelope may even be contrary to the general orientation of the overall idea of size (see also chapter 11 concerning level I performance on equidistances).

Under these circumstances, it is easy to understand the unidimensionality of goals. Almost all subjects of this level are able to shift from length to height and vice versa. But they cannot as yet consider size in terms of total surface—that is, coordinate the two dimensions in a simultaneous whole. To do this they would have to employ a mode of regulated composition, establishing relations between relations in the manner of a system of coordinates or, put another way, in terms of the relation of perpendicularity between the two directions. The case of Emi shows quite well that in a construction that is at once tall and wide, the elements placed sideways are seen as detrimental to size understood as superposition. In other words, this kind of composition produces in this case two possibilities. But it is not until later that these two possibilities can be united to form a coherent whole, a two-dimensional concept. This does not imply that regulated compositions will one day emerge as operations coming from a different source. On the contrary, one must determine how overcompositions gradually become regulated by the construction of relations between relations; that is, by the construction of higher order possibilities in the manner seen repeatedly in previous chapters. We have seen how co-possibilities come to replace sequential analogies, and more generally, how possibilities at first suggested by more extrinsic variations come to be inferred by a deductive process operating on variations intrinsic to a well-delimited system. Hence, the capacity to relate within a bidimensional whole (later three dimensional) all the variations previously considered one by one and in succession only certainly derives from this kind of organization of possibilities.

Level II

The fundamental problem presented at level II is to determine whether bidimensionality and the beginning of regulated compositions implied by it result from operations influencing from the outside the construction of possibilities or whether the reverse is true: that is, whether the initial overcompositions are regulated by an internal, autonomous process that in turn is the source of operations and their construction. Here are a few examples of level IIA:

Ser (7;8) begins by stacking up blocks in parallel; then, to do it "another way," he repeats the previous construction except for three blocks that he places perpendicular (one C+one B+one A) to the preceding ones: this gives a C at 90 degrees to a C at the base. The second construction appears to him bigger, and the reason he gives is that the perpendicular C *touches there* [the B underneath], which is not very clear. On the other hand, the two final constructions are the same as the preceding one made longer and the one before with superposition of three perpendicular structures. "Which one is the biggest?" *The other one* [the last but one]. "Why?" *Because I had mixed them all together, so it became bigger.*

Car (7;1) immediately builds perpendicular structures and even oblique configurations, then states that a simple stack of identical height is not as big as the other because *the other had more shapes.* This she says on two occasions.

Nic (8;5) also estimates as "bigger" a perpendicular structure, even though he did not use all the blocks.

Tri (7;11), after a simple stack of horizontally placed blocks, constructs another one with the higher elements protruding beyond the lower ones placed farther to the right. This second model of the same height as the previous one she considers *a bit bigger because there is some empty space here*, as if size was to be estimated from the virtual rectangular frame around the total construction, at least on the left side. Then she starts over again immediately, building analogous protrusions on the right side. "What did you do?" *I didn't put them too close together* [that is, build protrusions] *to make the biggest contraption one can imagine, but the other one I made was bigger* [=the same height, but more *empty spaces*].

Mic (8;6) first proceeds by length, then goes on to models of bridges, which she considers bigger the more empty space remains under the arch. Then she changes to another criterion: bigger *because there are many pieces*, spacing them as far apart as the connections permit.

After this come the subjects who refer explicitly to the two dimensions (level IIB):

Ala (7;1) first constructs a form with four levels, each perpendicular to the preceding one, and says that this contraption is *the biggest* because *it is big in width: it's long like that* [up-and-down gesture] *and like that* [flat, side-to-side gesture]. Then he makes a square and repeats the two gestures, adding: *but not big enough in height. I could make it still bigger but that would be difficult.* He then constructs a rectangular base with three sides of *C* blocks and the fourth with a *B*, then adds a kind of a tower: *It is tall and wide there* [*C* in front], *but not wide enough there* [*B* in back].

Myr (7;8) constructs first by length, then completes by height: *It's big this way* [side-to-side gesture=length] *and also that way* [up-and-down gesture]. She gives four further variations of the same theme but without mentioning width.

Ria (8;4) makes an enclosure | |, which she builds up in height: *It's big in height and in width.* The following six trials introduce many variations by overcomposition but do not go beyond her initial success.

Ana (9;0) begins with a construction like Ria's and builds a tower from *A* near the midpoint of the central line: *It's tall and I've tried to build it as wide as possible.* Then, after a number of similar attempts: *Oh, I have an idea, I could change it to make it better* [she does a kind of staircase]. *No, it's not better, because it is longer, but not wider.*

If we had observations on level IIB only, one might think that the advances in the procedures and especially in the two-dimensional interpretation of the term *the biggest* (with even some reference to the third dimension in Ala and Ana) result from the use of spatial operations. In fact, beginning at 7-8 years of age, subjects understand that to localize a point in a plane one needs two measures perpendicular to each other; that is, at this age begins the conservation of surface area. Having acquired these structures, it is to be expected that the subjects go beyond the unidimensional interpretation of the concept *the biggest*.

Yet, even if it is known that operations are characterized by regulated compositions and that this regulation is the result of progressive equilibration, as we have repeatedly tried to show, we still need to know how this developmental process operates, given the initial state. At level I, possibilities are generated by overcompositions oriented in any direction whatever and selected on the sole criterion of making something big. Now, the subjects classed at level IIA are of particular interest because they come to understand the relations present in surfaces or at least have a concept of bidimensionality, and this development is guided by a process that is inherent in the emergence of possibilities out of subjects' initial overcompositions. These consist at first only in deriving a relationship or a variation from the preceding one (at the mercy of observable effects produced continuously in the course of subjects' actions). These derivations take place in the successive-analogical mode; and, since the goal is to "make something big," all the successive variations and possibilities become coordinated in one direction so that the size of the construction increases in one dimension. These extensions can be made either in height or length, in parallel or perpendicular to the edge of the table, depending on the initial disposition. Whereas level I subjects, while speaking of "tall" or "long," simply go from one dimension to the other without relating them, thus maintaining a unidimensional performance, subjects like Ser and Car permit us to observe one of the general characteristics of evolving possibilities: that is, the change from the analogical, successive mode to that of co-possibilities, where each variation suggests several others simultaneously instead of only one after another in contiguous fashion. We can observe this when Ser and Car produce mixed constructions — incorporating perpendicular relations as well as simple stacks — which leads them to judge size in terms of this new possibility of mixed constructions, or of having built "more shapes." In other words, they have substituted a pluridimensional envelope for the earlier linear one. This change appears most dramatically in Tri and Mic when they arrange the blocks so as to enclose empty spaces, suggesting that the overall construction includes virtual borders surrounding both filled and empty spaces. Such reactions implicitly, but clearly, suggest that the concept of surface is present in these subjects.

The appearance of co-possibilities not only signals the change from the successive to simultaneous mode (although this is already a decisive progress), but also the formation of new types of possibilities that favor the development of regulated compositions out of overcompositions. These new types of possibilities consist in relations between relations, or relations between variations, which naturally pave the way for the development of operations. In fact, if it is clear that the initial relations and variations are formed on the basis of external observations, it is no less clear that the relations between relations give rise to a wide range of intrinsic variations that, when they reach equilibrium, lead to regulated compositions. If the subjects of level IIA speak only of "more shapes," of "mixing everything," or of empty and filled, the subjects of level IIB are no longer satisfied to use words like "tall," "wide," and "long," which may be ambiguous. Instead they describe their constructions by using gestures specifying perpendicular relations (already constructed at level IIA, but without conscious planning): now, the relation *perpendicular to*, as expressed here by gestures, is the prototype of relations between relations necessitating intrinsic regulation. This relation cannot be the result of simple, successive, and unrelated productions conceived of in the manner of overcomposition.

The formation of co-possibilities themselves has to be seen in relation to another important progress made at level II: the development of behaviors aimed at improvement and optimization. Behaviors that begin with subjects' immediate perceptions of necessary modifications later become anticipatory (preventing instead of correcting) when the subjects compare the new plans to previous results. When this happens, subjects have at their disposal not only a variety of successive possibilities but also an increasing range of simultaneous possibilities and choices. When co-possibilities lead to bidimensional constructions, subjects come to realize that it would be preferable not to choose only one dimension but to coordinate the two. This is illustrated in discoveries by Ser and Car that "mixing" everything to obtain "more shapes" permits a new kind of size concept, one that develops into the concept of surface.

Level III and Conclusions

The final level is characterized by two advances: the spontaneous recognition that size in general involves three dimensions; and the subsequent discovery of what follows from this—that if size is understood in terms of volume, then all possible configurations of the same 10 blocks are equivalent in size.

Rin (11;0) begins with a construction in the shape of ⌐¬, with some superpositions. "Why is this big?" *Because it is wide. Of course, one could do it bigger.* She changes to increase length. *Well, this time it's bigger in length, the other one was more like one block, this one is longer.* "One can do it still bigger?" *That depends whether it is in length, in width, or in height.* "What is best?" *A thing that's big everywhere* [she tries to find the right proportions]. *Now it's high, wide, and long; it's bigger than before* [by compensation].

Fab (12;2) still begins with the idea of height and builds a stack of 10 blocks, but with the following promising comment: *If I turn them upside down, that comes to the same thing.* From there she goes on to a *big and long* construction, then very quickly to a combination of the two: *Like this it is both high and long.* When asked, "Which is the biggest?", she suddenly has an illumination: *That one* [the last]. . . . *No! they're all the same because they have all the same surface* [=because the elements of the whole remain the same]. But then she is not sure whether it is the surface that really counts.

Den (11;0) begins by proportioning the horizontal and vertical elements: *It's pretty long and wide and high.* But having first agreed to try to do still better, she then objects: *One has the same number of pieces, it's impossible to make it bigger. . . . One could also make a really long train, but that wouldn't be high: since we don't change the pieces that always comes to the same.* "But comparing these two [constructions]?" *There is no difference: they're the same pieces, just put together differently.*

Top (11;1), after a few constructions of which he says *less high but longer,* concludes: *It's always the same system: length, height, width; but always the same size, because they're always the same Legos* [blocks].

Rem (11;2): *You can change it around as you wish . . . but it always comes out the same.*

Following the co-possibilities characteristic of level II, a new type of possibility forms, as usual, that is characterized by the notion of "anything whatever." The size of a three-dimensional, solid object cannot be changed because in modifying one dimension one necessarily also modifies the others. For a given fixed number of elements, all variations compensate for one another, conserving the total size of the object whatever the shapes created. To this intensional "any way whatsoever" there corresponds extensional infinity: "It always comes out the same," as Rem says.

Thus, it is clear that this type of possibility, which concerns variations intrinsic to a system and deducible rather than accessible through direct observation, coincides with the operational and structural type of possibility—that is, inferences derived by means of internally composed regulations.

The development observed here from one level to the next consists, thus, in changes of types of possibility: from that created by analogical successions to co-possibilities and, finally, to deducible, structural possibilities. The main characteristics of this development are then the replacement of the initial over-compositions by regulated ones and that of the earlier extrinsic variations by systems of intrinsic variations. All this finally leads to, as the conservation statements by Fab and Rem show, a synthesis of possibility and necessity, of the two components of developmental equilibration.

But as for the meaning to be attributed to these acquisitions, in terms of the dynamics of possibilities and their relationship to operational constructions, we emphasize that the earlier, more primitive forms of possibilities do not completely fade out at the upper levels. When the subjects of level III do not reason in terms of the whole system of compensations and conservations but attempt to realize certain particular constructions as examples of dimensions associated with various shapes, they proceed much like the younger subjects (except for a far superior degree of flexibility). Each construction, compared with the preceding ones, leads to a new idea of possible variations, which may be anticipated, conceived during construction, or thought of only after the fact. One observes here the same trial-and-error behaviors, the same scanning and more or less directed, exploratory moves.*

Two conclusions may be drawn about the relationship between possibility and operations. The first is that, at all levels, any variation introduced by the subjects will lead to others as possible ones. Different modes of generation appear at different times in development: analogical successions, co-possibilities, and deductions. The developmental changes are mediated by an increasing productivity in possible constructions.

Second, this increase in new possibilities—initially arising from overcomposition—sooner or later leads to regulated ones as subjects come to discover relations between relations, defining each variable on an abstract level. In this way, they add intrinsic variations to those derived from direct observations (this can already be observed at the level of co-possibilities). As a result, the second pole of subjective activity—the constitution of necessary relations between certain possibilities—comes to play a role. Operational structures thus appear to be a synthesis of possibility and necessity, as is well illustrated at level III, where the unlimited number of possible shapes is regulated within the framework of necessary conservations.

---

*It is not within the scope and purpose of the present volume to present in detail each subject's activities and productions (often quite long and involved), with all the changes in interpretation resulting from the procedures used, and with the resulting strategies. These topics are further investigated in A. Karmiloff-Smith and B. Inhelder, "If You Want to Get Ahead, Get a Theory," in *Thinking: Readings in Cognitive Science*, ed. P. N. Johnson-Laird and P. C. Wason (New York: Cambridge University Press, 1977), 293–306.

9

Construction with Sticks and Balls of Modeling Paste

with I. Flückiger and M. Flückiger

In this chapter we again introduce two situations, one using free constructions and the other goal-oriented ones. In the former situation we present small wooden sticks, cylindrical in shape and pointed at both ends (in fact, they are toothpicks), and very small balls of modeling paste (about 25 cm³). The toothpicks can be inserted into the modeling paste in infinitely many ways. In the goal-oriented situation, we use big balls of modeling paste that are said to represent bags filled with wheat. The task is to place them as high as possible off the ground to protect them from a flood (this can be done either by elevating them or by building a dam) or to protect them against rain (one solution is to build a shelter). As the goals are not narrowly defined, subjects do not really commit errors except for problems at the lower levels in estimating balance. Aside from this, there are no solutions that one could globally label as wrong. The formation of new possibilities proceeds in this case from attempts to improve constructions or to substitute one solution for another that may be an improvement or may be less adequate (such as a bad prediction). This task shows the relation between the formation of possibilities and problems of increasing equilibration (which has been analyzed before in terms of perturbations and constructive compensations); whereas the specific questions concerning possibility (which have to be further analyzed) concern the manner in which subjects become sensitive to the perturbation, after an initial lack of awareness, and increasingly demanding with respect to the definition of goals. Another important problem to be treated is that of deficiencies (or negative obstacles) as a source of needs (inasfar as they are felt) or of possible satisfactions. In brief, the definitions of goals and the kinds of improvements observed will lead us to an explication of the general mechanism of reequilibration, and their analysis in terms of possibilities and realizations will lead to a more precise understanding of the development of new cognitive abilities.

Level IA

Level IA subjects have difficulty in making corrections even in those situations when such corrections are relatively easy to make. For these subjects, it seems easier to increase the number of possibilities by constructing new objects than by introducing variations in those already produced—that is, by changing goals rather than by accommodating means:*

Nat (4;6) protects the wheat in *B* by building an enclosure of *b*'s tightly squeezed one against the other: *I can do it round or in a square*. She then decides to put a house and some people into the enclosure. The first figure is made of two stacks of three *b*'s each (*These are the legs*) united by another *C* on top: *That's the head*). For her second figure she uses toothpicks, which she tries to join on top by means of another *b*, but the construction collapses. She goes on to build the house, which consists of a *B* stuck on a toothpick with only a *b* as base. When this structure collapses, she adds a *b* to the base, but again it does not hold up. She then puts the entire construction on a new base, made of two *B*'s placed horizontally. In beginning another house, she repeats exactly the same construction that collapsed before. Then she arranges several *b*'s flat in a circle with another *b* in the center, onto which she plants a toothpick and nothing else. This inspires her to change projects: *I'll do a flower*, which she does by repeating the previous construction, except that the stem is oriented horizontally. *I would like to do a taller one*, so she repeats, for the third time, the *B* on top of a toothpick placed on a base *b*. Again the construction collapses.

Man (4;11), as a free construction, places two *b*'s flat on the table and links them with a toothpick. On each *b* she erects a toothpick and says: *This is a cart*. Then she decides to do a house. For this she puts down one *B* into which she inserts six toothpicks at the periphery. She concludes that this is *a sun*. She then tries a flower: a *B* on top of a toothpick, which she holds in her hand. "What if you don't hold it in your hand?" She places it on the table, with *B* as a base. *Like that, so it can stay up!* "Would you know a trick to make it stay up by itself?" *Yes*. She places a *B* on top of a toothpick planted on a *b*. The whole thing topples over. "But to make it stand?" *I shall build a house*. She constructs it on a plane, linking four *b*'s in a square with toothpicks. She tries to erect this as before with the *B* on top, which of course tips over again.

Oli (4;7), to protect the wheat, decides to build a house but begins with a human figure flat on the table. To make it stand up, he tries to stick a toothpick into the table. We remind him to use the *b*, so he links two toothpicks inclined by a *b* at the top, into which he inserts another toothpick horizontally for *his nose*. When all this collapses, he decides to change projects: *I shall make a*

---

*In the following examples, *B* stands for a big ball, *b* for a small one.

flower [a *b* with eight toothpicks around the periphery, on a plane]; *a sun*. "What about the flower?" *Yes, a flower* [he plants his construction on a *B*]; *it stands up like this*.

Pie (5;6), having built *an Indian tent*, has the idea of sticking three toothpicks on its top and putting the *B* there; but he places the *B* not between the three toothpicks, where it would stay, but stuck onto the end of one of the toothpicks, where it causes a general collapse. Instead of applying corrections or trying an analogous construction, he goes on to do *an Indian, a house* [a flat triangle], then a roof and a square, etc., but everything on a flat surface.

So far as goals are concerned, there is little difference between the free constructions (Man) and the responses to the instruction to protect the wheat bags. In either case, subjects jump from one project to the next, like Nat, who goes from his initial enclosure to the house, to people, to a flower; or Oli, who also ends up with a flower, which becomes a sun. This lack of *precursivity* (anticipatory subordination of the means to a goal) certainly plays an important part in the formation of possibilities at this level, where analogical successions are far more prevalent than accommodations and improvements. A second, essential aspect of these subjects' constructions is seen in the following: trying to have people, flowers, and so forth stand up vertically, they fail almost systematically in using to this end the toothpicks (except for Oli's final invention, arrived at partly by chance). Their reactions to these multiple failures, interesting for understanding the formation of possibilities, consist in preferring to give up the project rather than correct it. Only Nat, after having placed a *B* at the top and a *b* at the base, corrects by placing two *b*'s at the base after the collapse. Still, she never tries three or four; in addition, she repeats the faulty construction on two further occasions. Yet it seems a simple matter to improve the construction by putting a *B* at the base and a *b* on top, or by adding toothpicks. The problem may be formulated by asking why subjects at this elementary level find it easier to change projects and to realize a new possible goal by successive analogies than to introduce variations in their original project and thus to generate possibilities in terms of means and procedures, satisfying themselves with partial improvements without changing the design as a whole.

The most natural interpretation appears to us to be the following, which is similar to those given in earlier chapters (e.g., chapter 3). It has to do with the notion of pseudonecessity. Choosing a project or a goal means using the material at one's disposal to construct an object, which corresponds to a presentative, assimilatory scheme. This constructive assimilation, then, creates imagined and real objects whose properties result directly from the means employed (*B*, *b*, toothpicks). Modifying these means to correct or improve the construction, on the other hand, is to take the way of accommodation, but, as stated in chapter 4, of "an accommodative activity striving to find its form of actualization." In this case, however, accommodation is not simply imposed from the outside but has to be found and chosen. Under these conditions, if a presentative assimilation has not achieved its aim, it is easier to resort to a new one than to imagine accommodative variations in the model already realized.

Level IB

Level IB is characterized by an essential, functional advance in the formation of possibilities oriented toward ameliorations: the maintaining of goals or plans after initial failures and the search for corrections, which bear witness to a belief in the possibility of success. As a result, we find a first type of success: the construction of pillars with various kinds of consolidations. Here are some examples:

Lor (5;5) plants three toothpicks in divergent directions onto a *b*, then, upon examination, adds two horizontal toothpicks as support; he tries to place a *B* on top, saying, *I don't know yet where I shall put it.* When all collapses, he immediately sets out to tighten the three vertical toothpicks and carefully tries to replace the *B*. But he perceives the danger of collapse, undoes everything, and starts with a horizontal base made of two crossed toothpicks, on which he erects another toothpick with a *B* at the top, which leads to another failure. He then says: *I have another idea*, but, in fact, stays with the same procedural scheme: he rebuilds his base out of four crossed toothpicks, taking care to fashion a round *b* in the center (that makes a sun!); then he sticks in two toothpicks vertically *so the ball will stay in place*, and he even adds two more before positioning the ball. After this success, we ask for another system. He now takes two of the horizontal crossbars out of the base and attempts to place them as lateral supports. Since they are too short, he attaches them obliquely to the upper ball, *B*; but it *falls apart*. He still holds onto this idea and builds a base out of three *b*'s in a row and eight toothpicks (of which the fourth, fifth, and sixth are perpendicular to the seventh and eighth; the latter hold the *b* in place, allowing him to erect upon them three toothpicks in triangular configuration (a vertical in the middle and two slanted ones at the sides). This assures the stability of the *B because there are more things to keep it up*. This procedure with the triangle gives him the idea of combining it with the vertical pillar. The result is a construction with two levels with a *b* on top instead of a *B*, because otherwise *it might fall apart there* [the base at its center]: *there isn't enough modeling paste.* Then he inverts the levels: the triangle below, the pillar above, then, with a star-shaped base (17 toothpicks), he builds a construction of two, then three levels with pillars and inclined supports at the base.

Lau (6;3), when asked to do something about the flooding, proposes to construct a wall. She begins at the top, attaching two and then four toothpicks horizontally between a series of superposed *b*'s. She then tries to set this construction against a support in upright position. It collapses and she repeats the same project, but beginning at the bottom and pressing the balls hard against the toothpicks to hold them together.

Isa (7;6) begins like level IA subjects with a *B* stuck on a toothpick planted on a simple *b*. After this failure, she concludes immediately that one needs *many balls* [b] *and stems* [toothpicks]; *then you can put* B *on top*. But she does not insert the toothpicks tightly enough, and everything topples. So she tightens and crosses them somewhat, which leads to a success. Thus encouraged, she builds constructions of two and then three levels using vertical pillars, four *b*'s per level. She tightens the links as necessary but does not dare putting a *B* on top.

These reactions would be without special interest if it had not been for those preceding them at level IA, where subjects never tried to correct and accommodate their constructions. This sequence of levels IA and IB seems to show once again that possibilities do not originate simply as a state following another state, but essentially as a fiat developing in the mind of the child, who remains quite unaware of this potential. We observe that subjects confronted with their initial failure do not give up as do those at level IA but note immediately that they can improve their constructions. These improvements do not consist in changing the whole procedure (even if Lor says "I have another idea") nor in anticipating precisely what is to be done: they consist rather in the decision, tenaciously upheld (as in the repeated attempts of Lor at 5;5 years), that the original plan can be realized given certain corrections, even before they know which ones. There is here a kind of pure possibility, one that only furnishes the general framework within which successful corrections can be envisioned in terms of their outcome, yet still without provisions for determining the order in which these corrections are to be applied. After this, we see the emergence of hypothetical possibilities that characterize all attempts and that subjects undertake without knowing whether they will lead to success (Lor between his first and second failures). Finally, there arise realizable possibilities, as when children transfer proven means to new constructions, that is, differentiate the initial goals into new projects; or when they use new means but ones that are analogous to earlier, successful ones. The most decisive successes attained at level IB consist in being able to coordinate two kinds of means in new syntheses, as when Lor combines his pillars with triangular configurations.

We can thus observe a series of new developments in the generation of possibilities. They are no longer triggered by successive analogies (ignoring failures) but by a higher order mechanism, where the successive choices are determined by a purely dynamic possibility that consists in postulating that improvements are possible following failures. This development happens before subjects can even identify the type of correction necessary or invest it with hypothetical content.* Inasmuch as a failure represents a disequilibrium and the final success cor-

---

*It may be objected that children seldom verbalize their thoughts and that they may very well have particular corrections in mind once they perceive their failures. Thus it is not necessary to assume

responds to a new equilibrium, it seems therefore clear that possibilities in motion, which trigger a search for improvements before the latter can even be imagined in any kind of detail, are part of the reequilibration process. They represent its mechanism, which is both compensatory and constructive and is distinct from the states that precede and follow as the final states in the reequilibration process.

Level II

Whereas at level IB the observed improvements were necessary to correct the errors committed in trying to attain a particular goal, which the subject conserves, the improvements introduced by the level II subjects consist rather in completions or perfections: subjects no longer simply strive to elevate the ball *B*, but to place it on a surface. We can distinguish a level IIA where subjects simply attempt to construct platforms but do not consolidate them.

Mar (6;5) first puts up two toothpicks with a *b* at either end; these he links by means of a transverse toothpick, and then he adds two more horizontally so as to obtain a potential cube, which remains open, however. Mar initially believes this construction to be stable, but it collapses. He then puts it up again, completing the cubic shape* by placing other toothpicks symmetrically to the elements already in place. He perfects his construction by placing toothpicks in parallel over the upper surface and obtains a good table. He continues to produce tables, simplifying his structure somewhat by using piles of *b*'s for table legs and toothpicks for the tabletop, which thus supports the *B* adequately.

Pac (7;9) begins with a triangle that he changes into a kind of trihedral structure, but not a very regular one. This construction supports only quite light *B*'s. To support a heavier *B*, he first constructs a floor out of parallel toothpicks with a row of *b*'s at either end to which the toothpicks are fastened. Then he places four toothpicks, one at each corner, and turns the whole construction up so as to obtain a table. When the *B* turns out still to be too heavy he turns the legs a bit outward, which is a beginning toward consolidation sufficient to support one of the *B*'s, albeit not for the heaviest one. Pac then builds another trihedral structure, this time surrounding the base with a chain of *b*'s; he ends up by building pillars like those by the subjects at level IB.

---

that the idea of improvement as such precedes the particular choice that follows; the reverse may, in fact, be true. Indeed, in some cases the two phases of possibility—the purely dynamic, content free one and the hypothetical type of possibility—may seem inseparable. But it remains true that the subjects' spontaneous corrections imply the belief that improvement is possible and that this belief may remain pure motivation or in a conative state before it surfaces as conative behavior (hence the expression *accommodatory activity in search of its way to actualization*).

*For convenience, we speak of a cube not to designate a solid body but a plane elevated by vertical elements.

Mon (8;6), to elevate a *B*, arrives at an intermediate solution between that of using pillars and horizontal supports: she puts a *B* on top of a pillar made of four tightly joined toothpicks, then builds a second pillar equipped with several *b*'s at either end. These *b*'s she connects to the *B* by means of four more toothpicks placed horizontally. Thus, the *B* is not placed on top of a platform but attached to it by toothpicks.

At level IIB, subjects continue to construct tables. As soon as they perceive how unstable these tables are, they consolidate them in various ways:

Phi (8;6) rapidly builds a table made of eight *b*'s and eight toothpicks, four vertical and four horizontal ones. He then tries to do the top with parallel toothpicks but finds them to be too short. So he lays them across the four corners and then completes the top with toothpicks paralleling the four sides. But then, one of the legs coming loose, he starts a new construction, this time placing several *b*'s over two opposite sides of the top so as to attach transverse toothpicks. He consolidates by slanting these against the legs of the table. He continues with more constructions, such as a table with eight legs and a platform made with toothpicks placed in various directions.

San (9;0) builds the usual table and, to consolidate, adds inclined toothpicks at various heights, checking first to see whether they make a diagonal (at this age, many children still think that a diagonal is equal to the sides). Then she finds an ingenious solution: let the lateral toothpicks extend beyond the *b*'s on the top. This helps in two ways: two inclined toothpicks can be attached to the same *b*, and the tabletop is better covered with parallel toothpicks. Thus, the table is smaller but more solid. Still, her plan is imperfectly realized, so she adds further supports outside.

Ani (10;10) similarly builds a smaller table with a *tightly covered top*. She then goes on to construct a second level along the same principle, using two *b*'s for each horizontal toothpick and consolidating the lower level with inclined structures.

Level III and Conclusions

The transition from the various reactions of level IIB to those of level III is gradual and sometimes almost imperceptible. At level III, subjects discover that the most solid shape is the tetrahedron. This discovery becomes quite general at about 11–12 years of age, sometimes as a result of the slanted supports constructed at level II. The first case illustrates this transition:

Isa (9;0) begins with a simple cube, which she tries to consolidate by using diagonals. She finds the toothpicks *too small*. She then deforms the cube to provide it with transverse supports between the corners; this makes the construction more solid, but it *no longer looks like much of a square*! She tries to complete the system of supports and lets go of the toothpicks already placed. This suggests to her another project: *I shall make a triangle.* She builds it up and finishes with a beautiful tetrahedron, whose advantages she can see immediately—it is *more solid because there are fewer sticks and the balls have fewer holes: if there are many holes, they get loose.*

Ste (11;6) also begins with a cubic shape and completes its top with more toothpicks attached to new *b*'s, but he predicts that with really heavy *B*'s *it would collapse just like that* [correct prediction]. He thinks of slanted toothpicks, but *that doesn't work, because they can't go as high up as the straight ones.* This gives him the idea of uniting four toothpicks into a kind of pyramid, placing it in the center. *It's much like before, but the pillars are more solid.* He succeeds in finding the synthesis between cube and pyramid: four pyramids placed at the four corners of a square. Horizontal toothpicks placed on top make a regular platform.

Luc (11;6) similarly goes from cube to pyramid, but with five triangular surfaces; he also tries to find a combination with a flat top. His final production is a solid with two lateral surfaces in the form of a square and the two opposite ones in the form of a trapezoid. The top is then made with horizontally arranged toothpicks, resulting in the flat top desired.

Jos (12;5) begins with a square designed to serve as a base; but instead of going on to the cube, he replaces it with a triangle upon which he builds a tetrahedron as if anticipating improvements rather than using them to remedy the difficulties encountered, as did the other subjects. But he still wants to create a flat top, which he achieves by two complementary syntheses. The first is to surround the trihedron with vertical walls—that is, to create a kind of a cuboid around it with unequal and nonparallel walls. The second is its reciprocal complement—that is, to construct a cube that is then inserted in a system of inclined supports, which is equivalent to a truncated pyramid.

Gul (12;5), after the usual difficulties of consolidating the cube, builds three triangular surfaces; however, he does not join them to build a trihedron. Instead, he leaves the construction open on top to install the platform. Then he constructs a solid similar to Luc's to which he adds another one on top. The whole structure is reinforced by inclined supports.

After the essential discovery made at level IB that, despite an initial failure, the same goal may be reached with improved methods (which thus represents the source of possibilities as generators of accommodations), the reactions characterizing level II introduce a new type of improvement: they not only serve to correct a procedure following an unsuccessful attempt (which still happens, and even rather frequently) but also to perfect a procedure that obtains a more satisfying result. In fact, given the initial goal (elevate a *B*), this means introducing an intermediate form that we might call *new goal-means* (means toward the previous goal and the goal to be achieved by new procedures). This consists in placing a *B* on a platform to be elevated on a cubic construction of one kind or another.

The new achievement manifests itself in two ways. At level IIA, before the systematic tables of level IIB, the idea common to all subjects is that there are two ways of elevating a B: either one can elevate a platform upon which the B rests (or that the B is attached to, as proposed by Mon), or one can hoist the B alone on a pillar. This presentative scheme may not be particularly ingenious, but with respect to the problem of possibility it documents a new development leading to the state of co-possibilities—that is, a construction once actualized (such as a B on a pillar, etc.) is not only that what it is, but inasmuch as it can be seen as resulting from a choice, subjects realize that there was another possibility and even, once actualized, that there are still usable variations possible. The potential walls that Mar first builds can lead to a cube, and this may in turn get covered by a platform. The square base that Pac constructs can be turned around to become a tabletop or just as easily be reconverted into a pillared structure. As for the pseudotrihedrons, still badly put together, they are not further exploited because the subjects do not yet see what Isa comprehends at level III. This type of reaction can be observed on different occasions when an apparently superior model is rejected because of an incapacity to assimilate the relationships involved. Even the pseudoplatform of Mon evolves in the direction of a possible table.

In short, following the initial explorations of level IB—partly directed by chance—which are oriented toward a single goal, there gradually evolves a search for new variations that are seen as co-possible, which leads to the formulation of intermediate goals and of new means. Thus begins to evolve an internal dynamics of possibilities, whose principle is that each variation perceived (and a fortiori anticipated) becomes the source of still other variations. The associated production is guided by two kinds of mechanism. In weakly structured situations, the successive variations are related by similarities and differences combined (analogies), leading to ever new compositions up to the unlimited recursive series seen in previous chapters. In structured situations, each variation is compared with the preceding ones as well as with the goal to be attained (precursivity). This generates new relations that can be evaluated either as facilitating or perturbing. In either case, the new variations stimulate the formation of possibilities, which become more and more numerous. This then leads to two types of improvements: quantitative ones (only if the variations are equally useful) and also qualitative ones, permissible perfections and necessary compensations.

These improvements are evident in the reactions of subjects at level IIB, who do not limit themselves to piling up sticks and balls as if they could achieve stability by sheer quantitative additions; instead, they find clever tactics, such as reducing the dimensions of the table so that the toothpicks can cover it and keep the balls in their place, or reinforcing the perpendicular supports by oblique ones (without resorting to external buttresses).

At level III, a new type of possibility emerges, initiated by the consolidating force of oblique buttresses that are already used at the previous levels. At the present level, a new relation intervenes: reciprocity. Earlier, the buttresses only served as supports to avoid collapse; at level III, the three inclined surfaces of the trihedron are themselves supported by the other surfaces that they hold up:* In addition, we observe considerations of economy, as noted by Isa, and others concerning the length of the toothpicks (Ste), as well as the combined procedures of cubes and pyramids.

Thus, the development of possibilities has as its final achievement what we call *deductive possibilities* characterized by inferential anticipation and a progressive comprehension of the relations involved. But neither this nor the concrete co-possibilities seen at level II (that is, the simultaneous presence of possibilities between which subjects choose the one that suits them best) are to be interpreted to mean that this development can be reduced to that of operational structures. Nor can it be assumed that the composition of the new relations generated by the comparison with earlier variations can be equated with the compositions proper to the logic of relations and its structures. Rather, possibilities have a dynamic of their own, discussed as we just described; this dynamic is different from that of operations, which only concerns necessary relations and transformations (between real and possible states). It is the result of a kind of overdetermination leading to what we have called overcomposition. In fact, for each change that subjects introduce into the system of sticks and balls, they can observe a whole series of variables: their own movements, the figurative aspects of the structure, the precise definition of spatial relations, causal relations, and so on; and these observable phenomena may be comprehended to various degrees as a function of presentative schemes (including operational ones) as much as they may play a role in the determination of procedural intentions. There is thus overdetermination in terms of the factors between which all kinds of relations may be established, some of them relevant and others not. Out of this relational magma are born possibilities. Certainly, subjects do not retain all these relations, but those they do make use of result from an overcomposition that is different in kind from logical compositions, which are precursive and pertinent.

From this continuous formation of new possibilities, which look more like random attempts than planned constructions, subjects then select suitable hypothetical possibilities that can be actualized: this brings about the improvements that characterize progressive reequilibrations. We were able to distinguish three levels in the behaviors presented here: at level IB, possibilities generate new accommodations after a failure, with conservation of goals; at level II, we

---

*Earlier research has shown that 11–12-year-olds understand the causal relation involved in reciprocity—between *be supported by* and *support* in the situation with the castle of cards. See my *Success and Understanding* (London: Routledge & Kegan Paul, 1978), chap. 1.

saw possibilities as perfections based on arrays of co-possibilities; and at level III, possibility is conceived as optimalization, where the goal is no longer to produce the greatest number of different constructions, but rather the most efficient model (here the tallest) and the most solid and sturdy one. Note, however, that the two factors in equilibration – production of new variations and compensatory improvements – are not independent but go together from the beginning, becoming more and more interdependent in subsequent development. Right from the beginning, the overcomposition of relations is only partially random: it is at least globally determined by a motivation to explore what seems most interesting (in the sense of Dewey and Claparède). It is thus a kind of choice behavior, but it concerns mostly extrinsic variations. With the progress of improvements, choices still determine new relations, which are more and more centered on intrinsic variations. This *dynamic of possibilities* is what accounts for the functional unity of new creations and improvements (in spite of mishaps and local regressions). Even in the case of free constructions,* where the whole emphasis is on innovation, we observe improvement from one level to the next, improvement not with respect to the material results (which are all considered equivalent), but with respect to the way possibilities are generated: from analogical successions to concrete, then abstract co-possibilities and, finally, infinite, recursive series. But even just considering the actualized results, it is plausible to suppose that once subjects have found several different combinations, they may feel somewhat inadequate for not having found more (since the existence of n differences implies that of $n+1$). That is, when they discover new combinations, this may be a kind of compensation (in intension) toward intrinsic variations as well as an increase in extension.

As for gaps, which we have sometimes been accused of considering as perturbations (and of equating the bridging of gaps with compensations), the present study furnishes data that may be useful in answering that question. When subjects predict or note that a particular construction such as a pillar, a platform, or a pyramid is unstable and collapses, should we speak of a perturbation to be neutralized or a gap to be bridged? To be puristic, one would have to say that the collapse of a construction is a perturbation, whereas its timely prediction is only a gap. Certainly, one can only speak of a gap if the subject perceives it as such. For example, a physicist who knows nothing about the history of the pharaohs may not consider this as a gap. On the other hand, if the nonavailability of a datum hinders the solution of a problem and thus represents a need, this seems to us a perturbation like any other.

---

*In this chapter we did not discuss the results of this first type of technique, which was soon discontinued because it simply repeated the results given in chapters 1 and 2.

10

A Case of Deductive Possibility

with L. Miller and J. Retschitzki

In general, the development of possibility includes four levels. In the first, one variation leads to another by analogical succession. The second involves a certain amount of anticipation; it is the level of concrete co-possibilities, where subjects project variations that remain limited to those they will actualize. There follow abstract co-possibilities where the actual productions envisioned are only representative examples of a great many others. Finally, when co-possibilities become indeterminate, their number becomes infinite. This development shows a gradual progression from a state where the variations considered possible are generated one after another at the sight of the result obtained—that is, they are derived from external data. The final state of this development is reached when possibilities are formed from intrinsic variations deduced by the subject. We can, therefore, speak of deducible possibilities and their increasing importance with age and show how they result from a coordination of possibilities with necessities. The generality of this development has been traced in each of the chapters of this book, yet deducible possibilities have been closely examined in only two chapters: in chapter 8, with respect to the notion of three-dimensional size (volume), and in chapter 11, with respect to the construction of equal distance. But in both of these studies, the problems are complex in that they require not only the projection of new procedures but also an interpretation by the subject of the goal to be reached.

For this reason, it is useful to analyze the development of deducible possibilities in a simple situation where the goal is easy to comprehend so that it can be understood in the same way at each age level. We present children with several sets of six cubes or blocks of 3 cm^3, of which two opposite sides are empty and the four remaining ones are marked with a small red dot (occasionally we add some cubes with all six faces marked). A doll, also 3 cm tall, looks at the cubes from the side, and four tasks are proposed in varying orders: (1) the doll, while stationary, should see as many dots as possible—that is, the children are asked to arrange the blocks as they wish, in stacks or in a plane, keeping in mind that the doll cannot see the top surface; (2) the doll, also stationary, should see as few dots as possible; (3) the doll should see as many dots as possible while moving around; (4) the doll should see as few dots as possible while moving around. The interview always begins with a phase of free construction, enabling subjects to discover the various ways to assemble the blocks.

Level I

At the first level, IA, very few inferences are made in spite of the fact that such inferences are facilitated and even necessitated by the preceding observations.

Nat (5;8), for free constructions, arranges the blocks in squares, hexagons, semicircles, etc., each separated by a space. When we ask her if the blocks should stay "on the ground," she puts up a triangular building. For question 1, she lines up the six blocks with spaces between them so that the doll could see 12 dots. But it appears that these spaces are not intended for this purpose. They simply repeat what she did as free constructions: "How many red dots does she see?" *Six.* "How did you do it?" *Six.* "Can you do it another way so she can see even more dots?" *No, she cannot see here* [she points to the lateral surfaces, which are in fact visible]. "But you can do it another way?" *I don't know how.* Question 2: She repeats exactly the same row with the same spaces in between: "How many does she see?" *Six.* "Can you change it so she sees fewer dots?" *It doesn't work.* "There are always some dots to be seen?" *Yes.* We arrange the blocks in such a way that the doll only sees three dots. "Can you change it so she sees fewer dots?" *No.*

Cha (5;10) manifests slightly more flexibility. Following free constructions — vertical ones — he responds to question 1 by aligning four blocks with blank sides facing the doll and then placing two of these in front ⌐⌐, with the dotted side facing the doll; thus, in all the doll could see two dots. He then makes a correction, turning the other two blocks to expose the dots; thus, there are four dots visible, which he indicates one by one. "Can you improve it?" *One could do them like this* [he places them in a row but then changes back to his first construction, except that the blocks in front are spaced somewhat farther apart]. "How many?" *There, there, there . . . six!* "That's as many as possible?" *Yes.* "Try doing some more." He sets up a row of four with two blocks in front, placed so as not to mask the other two blocks. "That's more than before?" *No, six and six.* He finally decides on a single row but insists that it is best to combine the two systems (one does not see why). In question 3, he sets up a row of three blocks close together and three apart, but he counts only 12 dots, 6 in front and 6 in back (*the same there*), not counting the ones on the sides nor those on the sides of the interstices. "Another way?" He pushes them close together but does not expose any dots on the extreme sides. "Is that better?" *It's the same.* Question

2: He manipulates the blocks for a while and concludes: *Nothing to do*. "If she sees a few that's alright." He builds a row with dots visible on blocks 1, 2, 4, and 6. "You didn't forget something?" He turns them, exposing six dots! We show with two blocks how to turn them so as not to expose any dots. "Can you do that with six?" He aligns them, leaving dots visible on blocks 2, 4, and 6. "You can't do it better?" *No.* He still turns them with hesitation, as if he did not foresee any success, and finally offers no solution. "That's the only way?" *Yes.* "Try." He does another mixed row with blocks 1, 3, 5, and 6 exposing dots. "That's the best possible?" *Yes.*

Mon (5;9): Question 3: She places the blocks in a triangle but exposes two empty surfaces: *Oh! There is nothing here* [she turns one of the two, but still ends up with an empty side exposed]. *Oh! How will I do it* [succeeds with one side]? "Still better?" She puts them in a row but leaves the two extremes empty, then adjusts them. "Is that better?" *Yes, there are all dots here and here* [on both sides she has 12, counting the 2 that she adjusted]. "Try a bit more." Another row, but with an empty surface on either side. "Is it better?" *Yes.* "Why? . . . Where is it different?" Question 1: Agglomeration of five with one block on top. "How many does she see?" *Three.* "Another way?" [A row] *Six?* "Still better?" She spreads them, which prefigures level IB, but with no adjustment of the edges nor further exploitation. *She can see a lot* [eight!]. "As many as possible?" *I'm not sure I can do it* [piles up six]. "Is that a lot?" *Six.* "More than before?" *No* [the same]. Question 2: She puts up rows but only manages five, five and four empty surfaces, even though she attempts turning blocks to conceal the dots (in several places).

Jor (5;10), for question 3, contents himself with considering the two sides of a two-storied construction in which two blank surfaces remain visible even though it would have been easy to turn them around. In question 4, he begins with a row containing two dots in front, then builds a stack that exposes only dotted surfaces on two sides, undotted ones on the other two.

At level IB, subjects remain almost as inept at making inferences, but they discover the possibility of lining up edges:

Xav (5;10): Question 1: He begins with a row with dots on the six sides facing the doll and blank surfaces on top. "Is that as many as possible?" *Only if she cannot see on top.* "And otherwise?" He then builds two stacks, one with three levels, the other with two, using all six blocks. *Like that* [pointing from bottom to top, which he seems to interpret as "seeing on top"], *she can see two* [etc.]. . . . *She can see six, she sees a lot* [as if this was more than in a row]. "But she does not move." This objection gives him the idea to turn the doll a bit in its place and to do another row, but with the last block slightly advanced so that it touches its neighbor only by the edge. *I've turned the doll, so she can see everything that's going on.* "Is it better than before [than in levels]?" *No, it was better before, because she could see on top.* "Do you have any other ideas?"

I can always try. He then aligns three blocks by their edges, places two on top the same way and the sixth on top of the latter two blocks, with the edge facing the doll; this yields a total of 12 dots visible. "Is that good like that?" *Yes, 12, that's bigger than that* [one of his stacks of 6], *but it's the same as the others*. "How is that the same as the others?" *Always two dots* [he points to two adjacent sides on each block]. "But which is the best one?" *The last one, I think, but it's the same*. Then he aligns the blocks edge against edge. He thinks that this is good, but cannot explain why. Question 2: A block structure of three above three, exposing two dotted sides, which he reduces to one, then to zero. This feat does not get generalized to the following varied constructions, not even to one with five blocks in a row and the sixth on top. In question 3, he ingeniously disperses the blocks in disorder, which results in a large number of visible dots. But when asked to do "still better," his stack exposes too many undotted sides.

Jer (6;2), in question 2, builds a row of six blocks, of which three have dots facing the doll. *She almost does not see any more: only three dots*. "Can you arrange it so she sees less than three?" He starts over and ends up with two facing the doll. "Still less?" Reconstruction: one. *She only sees one dot*. "What to do?" *Turn them all* [correct: zero]. "Can you do it another way?" A three by two structure, but three dots remain visible! "And to have her see no dots?" Long manipulations, resulting in zero dots. "And another way?" He rebuilds the row correctly. In question 1, he makes a row of four, then six blocks, and says: *She would see a few more if she walked around*, which gives him the idea to place the last block edgewise against the adjacent one: *She now sees seven*. He repeats the procedure with a second and a third, which remain aligned, however: *Still seven*. But then he has the idea to separate them: this yields 9 dots, and 10 and 11, after turning each by 90 degrees. To obtain still more, he builds a column, alternating the orientation of the blocks: three blocks facing the doll, the other three with the edges turned toward her. This gives nine visible points, but Jer does not see his failure to generalize.

Ala (6;3), for question 2, presents a row of four blocks, with two blocks placed on top of two terminal elements: this results in six visible dots. "How did you know?" *I saw that* [blank surfaces], but this does not prevent him from leaving one or two dots visible in his following constructions. Question 1: Double row (two on four), with six dots. "Can you do more than six?" He places them in disorder, which only gets him five, so he builds a row of six. "Can you do it better?" *It can't be done*. "Why?" *I don't know*. "Why not seven?" He places them in a half circle, edgewise, but the blocks at each end (with two faces visible) have dots on only one of their sides, which gives six dots exposed. "Can you change just a bit?" He turns them and obtains eight. "More than eight?" He turns all the blocks so their upper faces are blank, which does not change anything. "Better?" *Ah, she can see* [on the blocks at each end] *two at the same time!*

He then aligns all blocks edgewise. *That makes 12!* "Is there another way to make 12?" *That's not easy.* He goes back to the half circles with eight dots visible. Question 3: Good construction, with four blocks separated and two apart with edges touching; this gives 21. "Do you think this is the most possible?" *Yes.* "I don't." He arranges them in a plane with edges touching, but in a closed figure, which results in a notable decrease.

These observations inform us about the relations between inference and possibility. The first condition that there be deduction is obviously that possible variations must be anticipated and not merely discovered in the course of action already initiated as an attempt. At the most primitive level (Nat), subjects arrange the blocks one by one with the dot visible; but after that they do not predict any more changes possible, even in question 2, where the number of dots is to be minimized. These subjects act as if one actualization becomes a reality excluding all other possibilities (the same reaction was observed in Cha when he first responded to question 2). A second condition on inferences is that any correction discovered as being possible by varying one element (e.g., rotation to expose or conceal a dot) ipso facto generalizes to other elements of the same construction. But the youngest subjects (Cha, Mon, etc.) only proceed by applying corrections one by one, and a local prediction never leads to analogous ones concerning other elements. This is a flaw in the co-possibilities at the most elementary level, that of openness within the same construction. The same flaw may reappear with respect to different constructions, one following the other (as in Cha and Mon at the end of the interview). A third condition is that subjects are able to compare different constructions built successively and to perceive them correctly. It is this ability that is lacking in Xav (in level IB) when he insists on finding still "the same [thing]" with two quite different constructions, such as a vertical and an edged one.

At level IB, we find the discoveries of new possibilities by demirotations of 90 degrees (edge in front so that two faces become simultaneously visible). Xav hit on this idea when it occurred to him to turn the doll around so *she can see everything that's going on*, whereas Ala discovered it when replacing rows by half circles. But despite these substantial advances (leading to optimal level I performance), these subjects still do not meet the essential condition for the inferences characteristic of deductive possibilities, which result from these prior acquisitions (Xan at level III and Jer with his final construction of a column).

In short, behaviors observed show in what way subjects fail to function at even the most elementary level of deductive possibilities; such functioning, totally absent at level IA, locally or momentarily prefigured at level IB, essentially involves the formation of co-possibilities envisioned simultaneously (where both advantages and disadvantages of possible variations can be foreseen). These co-possibilities must also be coherent with previous achievements (actualizations).

Level II

To attain co-possibilities by anticipation, it should be the case that deductive inferences are a prerequisite. How can we then explain these inferences in terms of advances in the development of possibility? The question to be examined is how it comes about that extrinsic variations drawn from experience and observation of facts turn into intrinsic variations derived by reflexive abstraction from the coordination of actions. Thus, since level II is characterized by the emergence of co-possibilities and access to intrinsic variations, these reactions need to be closely examined.

Vin (7;6) immediately solves question 2 with four different constructions of two or three levels; one exposes a dot in front, which he corrects immediately. "How did you do it?" *I put all the dots up on top underneath, and I put all the sides with no dots facing her and on the other side.* For question 1, he begins with a construction of five blocks (one block in back): *Oh, that's not the most. Like that* [four levels], *I can see all the dots* [six]. "All?" *No, because there are others in back.* "So?" Spontaneously: *If I do this* [one side turned to the subject], *I cannot see two at the same time, but if I do like this* [90 degree rotation, edge in front], *she can see two on each block.* He arranges six blocks in this fashion, on two levels, thus obtaining 12 dots. After several upright constructions, the last one two columns of two blocks connected by two blocks forming an arch (where all blocks are turned with edges facing the doll), we go on to question 3. He points to his last construction, saying: *She can walk around, then she sees exactly twice as many dots as before* [thus 24]. In question 4, he begins with two levels. Then: *Now I know: on the sides she sees nothing*, and he builds two rows of three blocks each, then attempts to do a T: *She sees three altogether.*

Mar (7;9), for question 1, starts out with a vertical construction, then disperses the blocks randomly; when he notices a block with the edge facing, he builds a column with the upper five blocks thus rotated, saying: *I think it's possible to have two dots on each block.* He then proceeds to mount several constructions where all blocks are oriented that way. "Is it possible to get more?" *I don't think so.*

Rob (8;9), also for question 1, arranges the blocks in a circle where six dots are visible from the doll's perspective (that is, the blocks are seen with the edges in front): *That makes six; that can't be the most possible.* He quickly arranges three plus three blocks edgewise on two levels. *That makes 12!* "Is that as many as possible?" *I don't know. Perhaps, if I tried this* [lengthwise], *that should be the same number.* He tries another column: *The same thing! Two dots on each block.* For question 4, he turns the blank sides out *so she sees more.* Then a row with dots visible only at the ends. In question 3, he turns this row sideways on its axis, which gets him six dots on each of the two sides: *Before* [in question 4] *it was the least possible. So, when I turn it around, it's the most possible*[!].

"Still another idea?" He builds a row showing 24 points. *That is really the most possible.*

Lau (8;0), who immediately succeeds with questions 1 and 2, makes an incorrect inference in question 4 (similar to that of Rob, whose inversion of the row is only partly justified); he interprets "the least possible number of dots" as "the greatest number of blank surfaces." Thus he aligns six blocks, saying: *She sees 12 sides without a dot*, which is true. Then he places three over three, repeating: *Twelve without dots*, which is also true. Only then does he notice, by counting the visible dots, that there are two in the row and four in the two-level structure. But after making allowances for Lau's interpretation of the problem (this happened with many other subjects), the co-possibilities he anticipates are evidently valid.

Olg (8;5), for question 4, constructs a row of six blocks with blank surfaces on each side. *On both sides, it's empty.* "Is that the least possible?" *No* [she assimilates, like Lau, the "least number of points" to "the greatest number of blanks"], *there are two dots* [at both ends]. *I would need a block with three empty surfaces.*

Pac (9;10), for question 3, furnishes a number of constructions in rows or with two or four levels, each time maintaining the "turned" orientations (at 90 degrees). He concludes without counting that *it's the same* and optimal since *each one has four dots.*

Sul (9;7) has the same reactions in question 3, *because she can see them all.*

Ste (9;8), for question 4 remarks that, with a stacked construction, *There are two more dots because there is another level*; whereas in a flat row one obtains the least possible — that is, *two, because on four surfaces there is a dot: it would take three blank sides on a block to make fewer visible dots.* Ste's final remark is already level III performance.

The differences from level I behavior are evident. At that level, a novel action became possible only as a partly random trial whose outcome was known after actualization and by taking note of what had happened. There was no prediction, only empirical conclusions, and no transfer to identical cases even within the same construction activity. In contrast, the subjects of level II do not act without some kind of planning, which immediately leads to the development of co-possibilities. For example, Vin begins by producing four different constructions in question 2 and formulates the principle common to these four (turning the dotted sides underneath and on top so that only blank surfaces appear on the sides). Co-possibilities, which are frequently observed in all subjects of this level, are of interest in that they represent inferences in *statu nascendi* since they imply, even without explicit formulation, a transfer from one possibility to another. Second, co-possibilities lead to anticipation of outcomes, which may or may not get confirmed after the fact; but they are not dependent for such empirical confirmation on the actual results produced. To be sure, an empiricist would say that such anticipation does not go beyond the domain of experience, that it is nothing but internalized or "mental" experience. Rignano proposes to explain all inferencing and deductive reasoning in this way. But he forgets subjects' actions, which themselves—and first in the form of mere possibility—generate inferences. For example, when Vin in question 1, remembering the dots in back, suddenly hits on the idea of turning the block by 90 degrees (edge in front) so that "she can see two [dots] on each block," it is this action that enables the subject to deduce the outcome, which is registered not by means of empirical but pseudoempirical abstraction.* In other words, it is relative to an effect produced by the subject rather than by independent changes in the object, which can simply be observed from outside. A new capacity that results from this process (barely begun at level IB) is the transfer of procedures, not only from one construction to another but also from one question to the next: thus, Vin, having built a structure with 12 visible dots in question 1, leaves it as it is in question 3, stating simply that now the doll will see "twice as many dots as before," which constitutes an elegant inferential transfer from one problem to the other. But even more is involved: the development of co-possibilities generates a new type of openness toward further possibilities, based on their very composition. For example, when Rob, having lined up six blocks with blanks exposed (in question 4), simply "turns it over" to solve question 3, he combines the action of lining up with that of inverting. This is a simple case of deductive thinking about possibilities, based on reflective abstraction (=abstracted from coordinated actions).

In general, the various advances toward possibilities as deductions show that the operational inferences and coordinations characteristic of level II constitute only one particular system within a more global one, which includes multiple possibilities that are actualizable through the formation of co-possibilities. The operational structures, which, once they are constituted, influence in turn the production of possibilities, thus appear as resulting from the more general development of possibilities, however autonomous and productive they become in the following. The reason we say that the operational structures are a result or a consequence is that possibilities, even or particularly the deducible ones, engender each other without limits in any direction whatever; whereas operational structures always incorporate chosen or imposed limitations because they are exclusively aimed at variations that can be coordinated in terms of necessary laws within closed systems. In this respect, it can be observed that necessary relations between possibilities are already present at the level of co-possibilities, as when Rob comes to consider 24 dots as necessarily being the maximum number possible.

---

*See our research on reflective abstraction. (Jean Piaget, "Recherches sur l'abstraction réfléchissante," *Études d'épistémologie génétique*, vols. 34–35 [Paris: Presses Universitaires de France, 1977]).

Level III and Conclusions

Two new acquisitions characterize this final level: the rapid identification of optimal solutions and, most important, their justification in terms of deduced arguments, which are explicitly presented as being necessary.

Xan (10;3) builds an optimal construction in question 4, a row structure. "Is it possible to do better?" *I think it's not possible. There are always one or two red dots showing. There are only two blank surfaces, and one cannot hide three sides. There is always one side at the end.* We can see the progress evident in this explanation relative to that given by Olg (8;5).

Teo (10;4), also with question 4: *Like that, one can hide more.* "One cannot do better?" *No, because she looks at the sides with no dots . . . except if one makes a circle.* He builds a large circle out of two sets of six blocks, blank surfaces turned out. *Still, she can see in between the blocks. It takes more blocks.* In question 1, he builds another optimal structure, a row with edges toward the doll. He judges this as optimal *because she never sees three sides.*

Bru (10;1) gives the same argument in question 1. In question 4: *The higher it is, the more she sees.* Thus, the optimal structure is on the flat plane.

These reactions raise the problem of the relation between success and comprehension. In the case of the four questions posed in this research, children clearly can succeed optimally without understanding the reasons. They can derive possibilities that take the form of extensional inferences or inductive generalizations. It may be that comprehension facilitates procedures and thus functions as a means. But the possibility is not to be discounted, as can be seen in other situations (see chapter 10), that subjects become so intrigued by the problem that they propose as a principal goal for themselves to come to understand it. In that case, the inferences used to this end come to play the role of means. The practical results are naturally successes, but they are seen as only secondary by-products.

In the present study, this level of success is already found at level II. But we also need to consider how subjects deal with the requirement of optimalization. Here again, subjects may achieve it empirically by noting that with different constructions results do not improve further. But to be really certain, they need to be able to discover the reasons and to subject possibilities to the relations of necessity and impossibility. In this case, comprehension plays a necessary role as a means to defend the optimal construction, the only way to be certain. Here deductive possibilities play a new role, that of relating possibility to necessity. In general, this characterizes the operational procedures and structures. Such capacities manifest themselves in certain simple situations (conservations, etc.) as early as level II.

11

Construction of Spatial Arrangements and Equal Distances

with E. Mayer and M. Levy

The following study has three divisions, which will be interesting to compare. The first deals only with free combinations: constructing a village out of about 20 rectangular buildings of various sizes and colors, including churches (and a tower), and a dozen or so trees, such as pines and apples. In the second part (and with different subjects), we present at first two houses and a tree, asking subjects to arrange these "so people can go and eat the apples"; then we continue with three, four, and five houses, eliciting multiple combinations by asking for them ("Place them any possible way," "another way," etc.). In the third part, used with all subjects, we ask for equal distances between the houses and a central point (tree, etc.), either starting immediately with 20 or 30 houses or beginning with 2, 3, 4, and 5 and then going up to 20. We complete this part by placing the tree near a straight river so that the distances are relative to a half circle instead of the entire circle. Occasionally, we also replace the initial phase by a modified procedure, using three trees and two houses (then four and five) and asking subjects to place them as they wish.

Parts I and II

The construction of the village has only produced one result worth reporting: the youngest subjects' tendency toward regularity and the search by 7- to-8-year-olds for differences. Here are a few examples of the first group:

Ana (5;10) places five houses in a tight row: *There.* She had, however, defined a village by referring to *many stores and roads.* "Could one build another one?" *Yes* [repeats the same construction]. "One might say that it is one single big village?" *No, because they should be together.*

Dom (5;6) is already halfway toward irregularity but apparently out of carelessness, with more or less curved lines that crisscross each other, and a group of pine trees in a corner.

Lui (5;10) builds two parallel rows of clustered houses, later united into a kind of rectangle.

Wil (6;0) seems closer than the others to differentiation: a long row of clustered houses with bits of two other rows joined perpendicularly to either end, plus a second long side that turns out to be an attempt at closure: *If I had more houses* [the pines are already placed between the houses, having been placed in parallel before], *I would have closed this completely or I would have done it all straight.*

Nat (7;5), in spite of her age, limits herself to a row of big houses (spaced apart) and another one with small houses. The trees are placed outside the village.

In contrast, we observe a clear trend toward differentiation in the following subjects:

Cat (7;7) constructs as many subsystems as possible of various shapes by combining houses and trees, *a church here, another one there, a stable, a bath-house. . . . She moves one house to another location. "Why?" Because there was already one like that close by.* Then another change *because it was too crowded there.*

Den (7;8) is similarly creative, building subsystems within a large circular enclosure (with the elements spaced apart). He points out *a customs station* (Geneva is surrounded by those!), and adds a few more complexes at the bottom of his previous creation.

Ang (8;4) applies the same principles but is not as inventive.

In chapter 1, we already noted the trend toward differentiation at about the same age levels. However in the studies presented in chapter 1, subjects had to find new positions for three dice under the instruction "to do something else," whereas here we do not ask subjects to build a village in all possible ways. The change we observe from regular, monotonic to differentiated patterns is spontaneous and has to do with the way subjects program their actions.

The second part of our research (where we ask for two to five houses and one apple tree that is to be reached, but without asking for equal distances) leads again to free combinations, but with the instruction to find as many as possible. It turns out that the analogical, successive procedures of the youngest subjects, which are essentially unprogrammed, except for a few short-term predictions from one figure to the next, still come to achieve a productivity comparable to that of the older subjects at the level of planned differentiation and give evidence of increasing inferential activity. It is therefore important to examine these facts carefully and to look for a suitable explanation for this elementary dynamic that produces new possibilities.

Oli (5;0) constructs 19 combinations with two houses in succession and then says: *Well, I've found enough,* then does 13 combinations with three houses, 19 with four, and 13 with five and six; but on the last trials he does not stop on his own. With two houses, *A* and *B*, possibilities are formed pairwise, more rarely in combinations of three: (1) *A* and *B*, one above, the other underneath the tree (*R*); (2) left and right; (3) in diagonal formation; (4) *A* and *B* vertically on either side rather than horizontally as in (2); in (5) he changes to *B*, *R*, *A*, saying: *Now it changes* (=permutation); from there he returns to solution 1 (6), but this time with *A* and *B* immediately above and below *R*, respectively; (7) the same, horizontally; (8) above and underneath; (9) on either side; (10) *A* and *B* at a right angle next to *R*; (11) underneath; (12) *A* and *B* form a bar right underneath *R*; (13) *A* and *B* superposed on *R*; (14) *A* and *B* farther away in oblique position; (15) superposition above; (16) like (10); (17) like (9), but with opposite orientation; (18) *A* to the left, *B* underneath *R*; (19) *B* removed from *R* and becoming contiguous on the other side in a vertical direction. It is undoubtedly this asymmetry that bothers Oli, so he stops there. With three houses−*A*, *B*, *C*−we find pairs and the third apart: — — becomes └┘ , ⌐| becomes |− , etc. With four houses, we find asymmetries or replications of figures (1) and (4–5), with duplexes *AB* above *R* and *CD* below, or more symmetries: squares, crosses, and so forth. Finally, with five and six houses, he adds stars and circles.

Ast (5;8), while performing similar variations with two houses, remarks about her 10th construction: *Oh, I've already done that one!*, which is not true, whereas Oli repeats the same figure twice without being aware of it. With five houses, she builds a curved arrangement and announces immediately: *And I can also do a circle with these.*

Yan (5;8) discovers a system that anticipates intrinsic variations but almost certainly does not result from any kind of deductive program; rather, it derives from simple analogical successions constructed one at a time: nine times in a row, house *A* and the tree *R* remain in the same position while *B* is rotated to the left above *R*, then to the right toward *A*, below horizontally, the same obliquely, then to the left vertically, then above *R* (produced before). Then he starts over with the first three phases without being aware of it. After that, he keeps *B* stationary and moves *A* around.

Pau (4;5), with two trees and two houses, places the latter between the former and then effects a few slight changes. With three houses, he puts the trees to the side and again effects only minute changes in the position of the houses.

Gil (5;8), in contrast, with two houses and three trees, arranges the latter in triangular or linear formation and changes the locations of the houses in eight different ways. With three houses and three trees, he arranges the former in rows or various triangular patterns and says: *Now I will change the trees.* He reproduces analogous configurations, but all are slightly different.

To explain this early blossoming of possibilities, we can undoubtedly make (as was done in chapter 4) the following more complex assumption: when subjects become conscious of a choice they make, and which is not imposed on them, they come to see the the the other terms not chosen as possibilities also to be realized.

Let us begin by analyzing the degrees of consciousness. When Oli constructed his first pattern (1), the decision he made constituted a choice from the observer's point of view, but not necessarily for the subject. If he had not thought of anything else, there would be no choice; but if, before acting, he hesitated between "above" and "on both sides," etc., then the action he carried out is the result of a choice, so that the alternative that was not chosen remains a possibility to be materialized in the next construction.* But if there was no choice at the moment of the initial decision, there is a second occasion during execution, especially if there is trial-and-error and checking behavior: when Oli places the houses vertically on either side of the tree, he can only hesitate between A to the left and B to the right or the opposite. In fact, he carries out both choices one after the other (4 and 5). Third, the subject's inspection of the outcome may well produce retroactively the impression of having made a choice: to cite again Oli's construction (1), when he saw A above and B below R and nothing on the sides, the obvious conclusion is that given this configuration, it is he who had wanted it that way. In other words, he had made a choice. The term not chosen remains as a possibility. When asked to "do it another way," he immediately responds by placing the houses on the other side (2). To assume that possibilities are produced by choices as perceived by the observer would be circular and tautological, since it would mean that the choice was made among possibilities already existing. Rather, what produces possibilities is the gradual process of becoming conscious that there are choices in other words, the emergence of the notion of choice in the subject's mind. This process is what produces possibilities defined as "it could have been or could be otherwise." A choice implies possibilities for the subjects who already know them, but it initiates possibilities for subjects who encounter them for the first time in the course of an activity. It may be objected that this too is logically circular. To this we answer that, psychologically speaking, there is a difference: in the case of possibilities we are only dealing with a psychological state, whereas choices are part of an activity. In this way we can explain the production of possibilities.

As for limitations, they constitute a second important aspect to consider. There are, of course, limits imposed by the situation and the task: "to look for apples" means for Oli that he cannot put the house too far away. But there are also the limitations resulting from pseudonecessities. Thus, Oli's first 18 con-

---

*In her studies on metalanguages, one of the questions Ioanna Berthoud asked young children was what the term *invent* means. Among the responses obtained, here are two particularly interesting ones: "That means that it's me who decides what it means" (6;11); and the second more synthetic answer: "To invent, that means *choose*" (6;8). See I. Berthoud Papandropoulou, "La réflexion métalinguistique chez l'enfant" (Doctoral diss., University of Geneva, 1976).

figurations are all symmetrical, and this is no accident. In this case, as in many others, the initial possibilities are limited by pseudonecessities. An essential condition for the generation of new possibilities is therefore the lifting of these restrictions. In our situation, this is relatively easy to achieve compared with that in chapter 1, where the positions of the three dice were to be determined in relation to differently shaped supports. When houses have to be placed relative to two trees, the situation also becomes more difficult (as with Pau).

In brief, the rich variety of the early analogical possibilities can apparently be explained with reference to an elementary process: that of a decision or immediate realization leading to a choice dividing the initially single goal into two analogical possibilities, the second of which is generated by the one that was realized first. Choice thus means accommodation, which, being essentially mobile, brings about a second one. Because the latter can be variously delayed in execution, an assimilatory schema can be established. Once this is accomplished, a new capacity is created that can be applied repeatedly, such as generating a series of possibilities. (This is nicely illustrated in Yan's developing a system.) Later this capacity develops into exploratory behavior and finally into more and more inferential predictions. Thus, at a higher level, the co-possibilities are essentially solutions simultaneously and equally "choosable." In contrast, the level I subjects only make successive choices.

First Forms of Equal Distance Constructions

As soon as we ask for equal distances between the houses and the tree, there are two kinds of choices subjects can make: one concerning procedures to be adopted, the other concerning the goal subjects define for themselves depending on how they conceive of the notion of equal distance. The earliest form this notion takes is to realize that there is a certain distance between the tree and the houses taken together even if the houses are lined up in a contiguous row. Thus, there is equal distance between the tree and each one of the houses for the youngest subjects.

Ala (5;5) builds a tight row of four houses perpendicular to the edge of the table. The tree is opposite the house farthest away from the side of the table. "Do people all walk the same distance to get to the tree?" Yes. "Could one place them differently?" Yes. He places nine houses in a tight row parallel to the edge of the table; the tree is again opposite and above the last house. We ask the same question as before. Yes. "And like that [we take away houses 3–6, so the only distances left are those between the tree and houses 1–2 and 7–9]?" Ah, no! "Why?" He puts houses 1–2 right next to houses 7–9 into a single, continuous row. Like that. "Other ways?" He builds an arc of a circle, which is correct, but uses only eight houses placed tightly together. "Could one put up more houses?" No. He has no idea of using a circle.

Tal (5;3) first puts down the houses in random order around the tree. The distances are quite variable. Then she builds a tight alignment, which is curved but not a semicircle, but it leads away from the tree. "And like that, all the people have the same distance to walk to get to the tree?" *Yes*. We take away houses 4, 5, and 6. "And like that?" *Yes* [but she realizes upon questioning that a boy who lives in house 4 would "win" against the one in house 11].

Cat (5;9) begins with two houses placed contiguously opposite the tree, which is correct, but then she extends this to five houses. "They all have to walk the same distance to the tree?" *Yes*. "And if they have a race, who will win?" *That one* [3]. "Another way?" She places the houses in a zigzag line. "But to have them all walk the same distance?" She lines up nine houses contiguously with the tree opposite houses 5 and 6. "Like that [question repeated]?" *Yes*. "How do you know?" *I'll put them closer*. She distributes them randomly but then goes back to a line with spaces between, placing the tree opposite house 3 and then 5: that is, she maintains symmetry between the two halves of the row.

Lau (5;11) builds a vertical line of three houses with no spaces between, the tree higher up and definitely to their right. When given more houses he continues his row up to nine, with the tree opposite house 6. When reminded of the task to build equal distances, he moves the tree farther away. This makes the inequalities less apparent. Following a second reminder, he moves the tree even farther, this time by a considerable amount.

Did (5;5), when given all the houses, arranges them in an ellipse. The tree remains outside, near one of the far sides of the ellipse: "Wouldn't some people get there before others?" *Those* [1 and 2, correct!]. "And to have everyone get there at the same time?" He changes the ellipse into an S. "And another way?" He goes back to the ellipse but places the tree farther away. With two houses and a tree he finds three correct solutions, only one of which is asymmetric. When given three or four houses, he no longer succeeds in achieving equal distances.

The notion of equal distance is correctly interpreted in the case of one tree and two houses (see Cat and Did). What, then, are the solutions subjects offer when asked to generalize to *n* houses? As soon as we go from two to three houses, Did adopts the strategy of placing them tightly, one against the other, whereas with two houses he once allowed more space between them than between each house and the tree. In general, subjects follow this strategy of reducing the distances between the houses as if they imagined that by condensing their configurations, they would acquire a general property of equal distance with respect to the tree. The simplest form of this solution is to create a vertical or horizontal row (A1a) and to put the tree near the end without considering the midpoint. Such alignments, even though they remain rectilinear, are conceived as a topological envelope so that there is only a single equal distance relation— that of the tree and the envelope. There is thus no differentiation between the individual relations of the houses to the tree (these become differentiated as new possibilities emerge). There is proof of this in subjects' responses to our subtraction of the houses in the middle (houses 3–6): Ala no longer considers the remaining houses as being equally distant from the tree because the envelope has been broken down into two different ones.

From this initial state, where only the relation between the tree and the envelope are considered, a series of new possibilities begins to open up and to get actualized. These derive from subjects' efforts to take into account also the elements within the envelope. (A) The simplest possibility is to replace the rectilinear configurations, where the distance between the tree and each of the houses increases linearly, by curved figures (Tal), zigzag shapes (Cat), or S-shaped patterns (Did). These can be seen as attempts to prevent the increase in distance between tree and houses. These attempts are, of course, not really successful (the houses also remain contiguous or very closely spaced). (B) A second strategy is to ensure at least that there is equal distance between the tree and two houses (1 and 2, 5 and 6 for Cat); the other houses are not taken into account. (C) A third method is to focus momentarily on the elements contained in the envelope by placing each house "nearer" the tree (Cat) in random order. This way the envelope is neglected (Tal and Cat), but only momentarily, with a changeover or immediate return to the alignment patterns. (D) The fourth procedure is particularly clever: from an initial linear configuration with the tree placed above or to the side, subjects remove the tree progressively farther from the envelope so that the inequality of the distances between the tree and each house becomes less and less apparent relative to the global distance (Lau). (E) A fifth strategy (adopted by Lau in combination with [D], and also by Cat toward the end) is to position the tree opposite the middle element of a row. In this way, equal distance is established not between the tree and each individual element but at least between it and the two half envelopes. (F) A sixth strategy results in a closed pattern (Did's ellipse). Combining this with solution (B), subjects achieve equal distance between the tree and the two houses at the extreme end of the ellipse; when combined with (E), the distance is equal between the two halves of the long side of the ellipse. (G) Finally, the most advanced possibility is to move in the direction of the circle by forming an arc as proposed by Ala near the end of the interview. Here the tree comes to occupy a central position with respect to the emerging curve, whereas in (F) it remains external to the closed form.

Intermediate Reactions

If we call the elementary level just described level IA, defining level II as that where subjects after a variable number of trials and errors arrive at the correct solution with the circle, we can distinguish an intermediate level IB, with interesting transitional characteristics.

A first group of subjects is characterized by a new possibility (let us call it [H]) that consists in separating the distance between the houses and the tree into two parts: a variable part, which is neglected, and a common part, which contains only equal distances and which is the only one subjects retain for their solutions:

Pau (4;5) begins as in level IA with alignments that have no relation to the tree, which he even moves farther away (as in strategy [D]). Then he arranges 11 houses in an ellipse, like Did. Like Did, he also notes that houses 1 and 2 at one of the ends are nearer to the tree. "What can be done to make them all have the same distance to walk?" *They have to go and get the others* [3 to 11] *all around, and then* [when they are all together at 1 and 2] *they all walk together to the tree.* In the following, he hits upon the idea of arranging all the houses around the tree but ends up in disorder. When it comes to placing the tree near the river, he only builds a rectilinear pattern instead of a half circle.

Die (5;5), after a random pattern that does not satisfy him, seems to regress back to the vertical rows as produced by Ala, with the tree near the upper end; but the idea is that *then all go there* [the house closest to the tree], *then they wait until everyone is ready, then they go* [together].

Ste (6;2), having built a closed curve, exclaims: *Ah! That's a circle!* This seems to be a first sign of level II functioning. But, instead of placing the tree in the center, she puts it a good distance away outside the circle; then, pointing to the center, she says: *They all go there, and then* [from there] *to the tree.*

These cases retain our interest in that they show new possibilities associated with a change in centration: subjects no longer consider the distances between individual houses and the tree (which they implicitly evaluate as unequal and variable), but rather a common, partial distance in relation to a general meeting point. Instead of the envelope, they now consider the elements contained in the envelope and their respective relations to the tree.* The most striking case is that of Ste, when he fails to see the equal distances between the houses placed on the perimeter of a circle and the center of that circle and focuses instead on the common distance between the center where the inhabitants of the houses gather and the tree, which is placed outside of the circle.

A second method (I) for going from the initial relation of tree ⟷ envelope to more differentiated possibilities is to break down the total envelope into partial ones. These are arranged in any order whatsoever, therefore not in symmetrical patterns. Two conditions, however, are generally respected: there is equal distance between each of the houses within any one of the partial envelopes and

---

*This solution has a certain analogy with *categorial products.*

the tree; and there is equal distance between each one of these different partial envelopes and the tree:

Ern (5;5) distributes the houses in four rows (a to d) of two to five elements, with also a small, closed figure (e); the tree is in the center of these configurations, which are distributed without symmetry or parallelism (in various orientations). "In this case, does each inhabitant walk the same distance toward the tree?" Yes, those [nine houses, in spite of their increasing distance from the tree]. "And others?" Yes, all those [b or four houses arranged in an oblique line, and c]. But in comparison with c (five houses in a still more oblique line), the people from b do not walk as far because they are too close. He moves them a bit farther away: Now it's the same.

Dom (5;6), after having built single rows, groups these in vertical columns above the tree and concludes: They all walk the same time.

Wil (6;0), after having created horizontal rows, breaks these up into three and four parallel subdivisions in immediate proximity. He builds an enclosure all around and inserts the tree in the upper row: he considers all these multiple, tightly spaced (laterally and vertically) houses as being equally distant from the tree. This also applies to each of the rows.

These solutions (I) are carried further as (J): here, the partial envelopes get arranged symmetrically or in circular patterns with the tree in the center:

Lui (5;10) begins with straight rows, the tree opposite the midpoint (as in [E]), but from there he progresses toward symmetrical patterns by building two vertical rows with the tree in the middle opposite house 3 in each row of seven houses; this yields a doubly symmetrical pattern within and across rows, a prefiguration of later square or circular patterns. True, he does not by himself attain these, but he understands their rationale when we propose them. Before any suggestion from us, he places the houses as endpoints of two midlines of a square (i.e., $+$) and of two diagonals ($\times$). The result is a square configuration containing two kinds of correct equal distances, which are, however, not equal to one another.

Suz (5;6) begins with up to six houses, which she arranges symmetrically around the tree. But in trying to arrange the whole set, she only builds large, asymmetric, ovoid patterns, with the tree enclosed but not central. After this she divides the whole into five partial, rectilinear configurations of four or five elements, arranged as a star pattern with the tree in the center. She believes that there is equal distance between the houses and the tree.

It is clear that solutions (H) to (J) are attempts to differentiate the global relation of the tree to the envelope into equal distances between it and individual houses. Since this does not succeed, a few subjects think of a possibility (K), which consists in suggesting blatantly that one multiply the number of trees even up to one per house, which would easily create equal distances without having to resort to subconfigurations:

Cec (5;8), although able to do a circle with seven houses and finding solutions of type (I), still concludes: *There are not enough trees*, indicating the need for one tree per house.

Cat (7;7) (cited in the first section above) builds a rectangle to assure equal distances, but she notes that there are still inequalities in getting to the tree in the center. So she puts a tree in front of each suite of two to three houses. *I still need more trees* to put one in front of each house.

Pie (7;4), beginning with symmetries of type (J) like Lui, is dissatisfied: *No, one would need several trees*, and indicates where to put them—one in front of each house.

But the most common solution in these intermediate cases is to combine the envelope in the form of a closed figure (L), with equal distances separating the tree in the center from the houses at the periphery (in contrast to solution (F), where the tree remains outside of the circle). Among these closed figures we may find the circle, but subjects do not as yet understand its particular relevance:

Jer (4;5) first scatters the houses around the tree, then builds *a round* with the tree in the center. But then he adds three more houses, refusing to remove them from the circle: *No, they need to be inside the round.*

Jan (5;3) begins by placing 2, 3, 4, and 5 houses around the tree, which suggests to her the idea of a circle when she has 20 or 30. The circle she then replaces by a square, a triangle, a rectangle, and a kidney-shaped figure, each time affirming that there is equal distance between the houses and the tree.

Oli (5;0), whose 18 symmetrical shapes with one tree and two houses, etc. (achieving some equal distances even up to 5 and 6 houses) we described above, begins to build semicircular and semisquare patterns with 20 houses (without closure and with one oblique side). Then he builds a circle with a crescent shape inside, after which he constructs a perfect circle, which he soon replaces by a rectangle. In spite of the fact that he had noted when considering the open figures that some houses are *too far*, he claims equal distance for the long rectangle.

Yan (5;8), with four houses, places these at the extremes of diagonals $\times$ or medians $+$, which are both correct solutions. But when given a greater number of houses, he places them in a square pattern, unaware that there no longer is equal distance for all houses. Then he replaces the square by a circle, but he unfortunately completes this by putting four houses inside—two (*ab*) lined up next to each other and two others (*cd*) in a V. He first declares that there is equal distance between *ab* and *cd*, which is not the case, then between *ab* and *cf* (situated on the wide circumference), which is even less true: "Is it exactly the same distance to walk?" *No.* "Where would they walk the farthest?" *I do not know.*

Pac (5;8) arranges 20 houses in pairwise patterns ($+$, $\times$, etc.), but in concentric circles at increasing distances: *They have almost all the same distance to walk*; as the distances get more and more unequal, he can see that one *walks farther*.

Tie (6;3) begins with a simple row, the tree placed at the midline. Then he goes on to the rectangle, the tree in the center: he first affirms that there is equal distance for all, but then acknowledges inequality when comparing a house very near with another one quite far away. He then discovers gradually an arrangement with the tree midway between four tight agglomerations, two vertical and two horizontal ones. He believes he has thus found equal distances for all elements, in spite of the greater distance for the houses at the far ends. With the tree near the river, he offers a simple line as well as a triangle, but he does not find the solution with the semicircle.

And (6;0) begins with a square, then builds irregular shapes that are open or closed. Only the latter are thought to assure equal distances.

What is interesting about these facts is the difficulty subjects have in differentiating possibilities when this requires a liberation from an initial pseudonecessity. In this case, the latter consists in a falsely assumed equivalence of the distance relations between two or n pairs of houses and those between envelopes or configurations (rows, curves, closed forms). These false inferences, which are characteristic of the most primitive level described earlier, are partially eliminated as soon as the new possibilities (H to K) single out certain kinds of correct equal distances. But with the closed figures of type (L), where the tree is placed in the center and no longer outside, the difficulty reappears. Certain kinds of equal distances E_1, E_2, etc., between pairs of particular elements (for example, between the corners of the cross configurations $+$ or $\times$) are discovered individually and then generalized across patterns, where in fact there are no equal distances. That is, from the fact that these individual equivalences are contained within a larger configuration, $E_1 + E_2 + \ldots = E$, subjects consider them as similarly equivalent, $E_1 = E_2 = \ldots$ They cannot as yet conceive the only possibility to equalize them, which is to create a circumference with only the tree in its center. They already consider this possibility but only momentarily, and they do not understand it as the only possible solution. From the point of view of the growth of possibilities, these reactions show a lack or a deficiency of differentiating the possible from the impossible: the envelope thus constitutes a source of virtual perturbations, which will have to be compensated by anticipations (we say *virtual* because the envelopes lead to false equidistance relations only in certain cases and not through pseudonecessities, at least for level IB).

Levels II and III

Starting at 7–8 years of age, subjects find the solution of the circle but only after trial and error through successive actions, which lead them to see that only the "round" pattern ensures equal distances:

Mat (6;8) is interesting for his repeated corrections. Beginning with a square, he corrects it to a circle, followed by a star pattern with the corners at equal distances from the center. With the tree by the river, he begins the same way with half squares, which he corrects to half circles. Going back to the tree without the river, he starts with rectangles, which he corrects again to a circle: *Like that they all arrive at the same time.*

Nat (7;5) also begins with a square: *They have the same distance to walk.* "How about that one [near a corner] and that one [midpoint of the side]?" *No.* Then she forms a nice circle with houses noncontiguous. "And those [the small ones]?" She inserts them between the other houses but not in the center, as do the level IB subjects. We move one house nearer the tree. "Show me how to get it so that all have the same distance to walk." She moves the other houses closer to the tree, building a smaller circle.

Van (7;9) starts with a curve that does not make much sense, which he then makes a bit rounder: "They have the same distance to walk?" *No.* Then he builds a nice circle, houses closely spaced. We add more houses and he places them in an arc outside of the circle, then, to equalize distances, he enlarges it, incorporating all the elements of the previous circle. With the half circle against the river, he proceeds by approximations.

Axa (7;11) remarks immediately: *I put them around*, but he builds only a half-circular, half-linear configuration. He corrects this to a circle but also tries a square, having certain doubts, however (*I don't know if that works*). When he sees the outcome, he says immediately: *No, there* [in the corner] *they are farther away.* This does not prevent him from starting the same way for the tree by the river, correcting afterward to a semicircle.

Kar (7;2), for two and three houses, puts them up in a straight line; for four houses she corrects to an arc, and for the whole set builds a circle *all around the tree.* She proposes as another solution to condense it to an arc or to space them wider apart for a larger circle.

Ang (8;5) immediately finds the circle solution, and when asked to add more houses he refuses (with good comprehension) to put them inside, since those *would have less far to go.* But he comes up with the strange idea of leaving a portion of the circumference empty and of arranging the new houses in a similar arc farther away from the center. Only then does he exclaim: *Ah, no! they don't have the same distance to walk!* He then builds a large circle. When asked to do "something else" equally correct, he builds seven discontinuous arcs at the same distance from the center.

Car (9;8), after a few errors with three trees and three houses, proceeds to build arcs. When given all 20 houses, he arranges them immediately in a circle. To do something else, he arranges them in a star pattern, tries a cross pattern with closely spaced elements, noting: *No, that doesn't work.* He then goes back to the circle but alternately places houses perpendicularly as radii or extends these beyond the circumference: *That's like a sun with rays.* "Can it be done still differently?" *No, I don't think so.* "And the square?" *No, that's not possible.*

Joe (10;7), after having built a circle, still says: *I'll try a square* [does it]. *No, the corners would be farther away.* "Why did you do a square, after all?" *I just wanted to be sure.*

Level III only begins by 11–12 years of age. It is characterized by two new acquisitions: the anticipated necessity of the circle, which is therefore deduced and not simply found after the fact; and the infinite extension of possibilities but only in the sense of variations of the circle:

Cla (11;1) at first sees as only possible variations that of *enlarging the circle.* When pushed further, he replies: *I think there are others, but. . . .* He then places the houses in a star pattern, etc., always referring to the corners.

Cri (11;9) proposes *a round.* "Could it be done another way?" *No, but one could arrange the houses another way* [he arranges them in a star pattern], *but the form* [circular] *would be the same.* Or else: *I might enlarge the circle,* and this could be done in infinitely many ways.

Compared with level II, where subjects still need to check things out (as Joe did at 10 years) to verify that only the circle guarantees equal distances, certainty becomes inferential at level III.

Conclusions

Unlike the free combinations required in part II of our research (see Oli to Gil, above), where all solutions are correct so long as they are different, the possibilities to invent in order to solve the problem of equivalence not only can lead to successful or unsuccessful performances but, in addition, require modifications in the concept of equidistance itself (or in its presentative schema). Accordingly, we find transformations from levels IA to III. The first question is then to determine whether this development of possibilities results from development of the spatial schemata and their operational structures.* Or, as in the task of constructing triangles (chapter 12), the improvements on the procedural level could explain the increasing precision in equal distances seen as goals corresponding to the procedural means employed.

When comparing children's solutions from one end of the developmental scale to the other (for example, Ala's crowding of nine houses into a tight row with the tree at the extreme end, above the last house, in contrast to the circles produced at level III, with the tree in the center), we observe a complete reversal. At the initial level, the houses are considered to be at equal distances from

---

*We once studied this issue with B. Inhelder, with special emphasis on the notion of equal distance. See J. Piaget, B. Inhelder, and A. Szeminska, *The Child's Conception of Geometry* (New York: Basic Books, 1960).

the tree because they are seen as being located within a single envelope and hence as participating in an identical distance relation between this envelope and the tree, which is located anywhere outside the envelope. At the final level, the houses are seen as being located at equal distances from the tree because they form an envelope around the tree, which occupies the center. Thus, the houses create a co-envelope function in regard to the tree. This complete reversal from the use of co-enveloped to co-enveloping elements seems to result at least as much from an evolution of procedures as from that of presentative schemata. Therefore, the relations between the two mechanisms will be all the more amenable to analysis.

If we want to present a schema of the sequence of procedures and the new possibilities that they generate one after the other, we can compare them to a tree whose height represents levels of growth that are independent of the lateral branches not having the same regularity. In other words, among the phenomena described in the three preceding sections, we can distinguish sequential from occasional possibilities. The occasional ones, such as that of pairing a tree to each house (in Cec, Cat, and Pie), we shall ignore. The main developmental steps can then be seen to consist in seven distinct levels: (1) Line up the houses in closely spaced rows without regard to the tree; (2) move them nearer to the tree by various means (curves, etc.); (3) introduce symmetries by placing the tree either opposite the midpoint of a row or between the medians of two partial envelopes (linear, etc.); (4) give up these simple symmetries in favor of multiple ones grouped "around" the tree: for example, at the extremities of two potential crosses, $+$ and $\times$; (5) enclose the tree by means of houses arranged in closed, regular figures (squares, rectangles, circles) with the tree in the center (as in [4]); (6) control all distances between each individual house and the tree, which is easier to do with a closed figure, whose borders can be perceived simultaneously, than in any other comparison ($x \rightarrow y$ compared with $x' \rightarrow y$): as is well known, young children estimate length in terms of the endpoint rather than the intervals between the two extreme points; (7) correct evaluation of equal distances. The result is a common envelope formed by the houses around the tree, the equalization of all individual distances between each house and the tree (with four houses and even five, the distances often remain unequal), and the restriction to the circular form (as asserted at level III). Thus, the great variety of possibilities envisioned up to this level gets reduced to a single type: in exchange, this sole survivor gets endowed with the notion of intrinsic necessity.

If this interpretation is correct, we can first conclude that each possibility opens toward the following one in the usual way—by analogy, contrast, completion, and so forth. This involves correction of errors as well as discovering new relationships and means. Second, we observe that the invention of new means most often leads to new goals, which in turn generate new means. Thus, we saw how subjects add or substitute curved configurations for the linear ones used exclusively before so that the houses get closer to the tree; the relation of *nearer* then suggests the symmetries, which later become extended to that of *around*.

Further, it is apparent that this development cannot be explained only as one of operational generalization, since in the kind of goal-oriented situations we study subjects choose procedures because they judge them to be better than others, which are discarded (including the ones previously used). In these situations, subjects can have successful or unsuccessful solutions (all this is very different from the generation of new possibilities in the situation of free combinations, which we described above in the first section). Keeping in mind the fact that operational schemes are both procedural and presentative and reserving the term (presentative) *generalization* to mean construction of new structures (as opposed to the solution of particular problems), there remains a clear-cut difference between this operational generalization and the generation of new procedural possibilities: whereas the former is grounded in what precedes—the structures already existing—and goes in the direction of greater recursivity, but without being oriented toward a specific goal, the latter corrects what precedes by selecting means toward a particular goal already present from the outset (precursivity). The production of new possibilities thus proceeds by correcting and completing previous ones to the extent that goals become more clearly defined in the process, which in turn stems from the means used to attain these goals. Two consequences follow from this: first, the preceding possibilities become "impossible," being erroneous or incomplete; second, when a goal is better defined and comprehended it becomes more attainable to the extent that the means come to be more adequate. In other words, completing a defective procedure is very different from a completive generalization: it means correcting errors with regard to a goal, which is itself better defined (recall the failure to realize equality of distances at developmental steps 4 and 5), whereas a completive operational generalization (such as the change from *groupings* to *part-whole* structures) incorporates what precedes without modifying or rejecting anything, and even without anticipating the outcome of the completion (the properties of the new structure). On the other hand, as soon as a goal (better defined and made successively more precise and more realizable) has been attained by equally improved procedures (reducing the distance between means and ends), the obtained result becomes justifiable and demonstrable by processes of constructive operational generalization that are different from the heuristics used to attain it. These novel processes subordinate the only possibilities finally retained to the relations of intrinsic necessity.

In general, both the remarkable number of possibilities characteristic of levels I and II and their interrelations in terms of spontaneous derivations seem to point to the essential role of this procedural development as a general framework within which operations are constituted by progressive coordinations of possibilities and necessities.

12

The Construction of Triangles

with I. Berthoud-Papandropoulou and H. Kilcher

The construction of all possible triangles raises a problem that is central to our concerns—that of the relation between the procedural and the presentative schemes, between procedures and operations, between analogical and deduced possibilities, and, generally, between extrinsic and intrinsic variations. As far as the latter half of these relations are concerned, subjects of more advanced levels can, from the fact that a triangle has three angles and three sides, deduce the following facts: that the sides can be of equal lengths, either all three of them or just two; or that all sides may be unequal; further, that the angles may also be equal or unequal, hence the possibility of a right angle, of isosceles or scalene triangles. But it is not our concern here to analyze the operations that enable subjects to make such inferences late in development; rather we want to study, age by age, the procedures used to build, by means of various materials or by drawing, "all possible triangles," or what are deemed such by the subjects. Since any procedure consists in means toward an end, our study will be directed at once at the goals subjects give themselves (the way they conceptualize the various forms of the triangle), the means they use (which turn out to be more informative than expected), and the relation between means and ends. These relations are particularly interesting with respect to the question of the emergence of new possibilities, because as much as a particular goal can be reached by various means, so one and the same means can lead to new goals. These relations are not symmetrical, and they extend outside of the initial system, with the result that new possibilities open up. Thus, this research on "all possible triangles" concentrates on a problem domain that lies far outside of that treated in operational analysis, even though the structures in question lie within the latter domain.

Materials and Methods

The interview (of variable length, depending on subjects) includes five parts. In part 1, we present children with six pieces of spaghetti, of which three are equal

123

in length and the others unequal: *a, b, c, d* (a=15.5 cm, d=6.5 cm). The instructions are to "make some shapes," then to "make triangles"; followed by "make another one," "a different one," "a very different one," etc. With the materials, one can make equilateral, isosceles, and scalene triangles. It is acceptable to use more than one element on each side (in that case, we call them *composites*).

In part 2, we present two long pieces of spaghetti (22 cm) and begin by asking subjects to use these to "make a triangle" (this surprises the youngest subjects). If necessary, we suggest that the spaghetti be cut to construct the triangle. Then we present two more pieces of spaghetti with the instruction to "use them up" so that there will be "nothing left over" (as is often the case at first). Finally, we only present one piece of spaghetti with the same restrictive instruction. Thus, the idea is to get the child to adjust the length of the pieces so as to use them as sides in a triangle (which offers a great many possibilities).

In part 3, we present the child with a circular piece of steel wire, closed to a ring, on which are strung three pearls. The instructions are to make a triangle by bending the wire (we also ask what the pearls may be good for), then to make other triangles and to say how each triangle is different from the previous ones. The purpose of this task is to offer the child an occasion to create various sides and angles freely and to modify them within certain fixed limits (the length of the perimeter). We further wish to gather information concerning the transition from one to another type of possibility. This information will be both behavioral and verbal: observations on how children go about bending the wire and on how they explain their actions verbally.

In part 4, the material consists of five wooden sticks of different lengths (a=17.5 cm, b=13.5 cm, c=7.5 cm, d=6.5 cm, and e=4 cm). Again the instruction is to construct as many different triangles as possible. If a child uses more than three elements for the first triangle (a composite one), we ask for a construction with only three sticks ("another one," "a different one," etc.). It should be noted that equilateral and isosceles triangles cannot be constructed with this material. Nevertheless, there are degrees of approximation to these prototypic forms: the triangle *cde* (out of small elements), the triangle *abc* (large elements), and the triangles *bcd* and *abe* (very heterogeneous elements), which are near the limit of a triangle. In addition, certain combinations cannot be used in the construction of triangles (*acd, ace, bce,* and *bde*). Pretending to try to play a trick on someone, we ask the children: "Choose three sticks with which it is impossible to make a triangle." The purpose is to analyze what children at different developmental levels consider impossible—the limits and the complementary sets of possibility—and to study how they demonstrate impossibility in action.

In part 5, we ask children to draw all possible triangles. This task is used to compare performance under material constraints to that in the free graphic situation.

Preliminary Schemata

In this section we present cases where the subjects have not yet developed presentative schemes incorporating the triangle (their schemata are limited to closed figures that are either rounded or quadrilateral). These subjects can produce, only with great difficulty, approximate copies of triangles presented as models to be reproduced with the spaghetti or by drawing:

Lis (4;5), with the spaghetti pieces for part 1, builds a rectangular "park" of which three angles are carefully closed and the fourth left open (due to unequal lengths on the long sides); she repairs this with an obliquely positioned piece. When asked to do it with three pieces (*c* of part 1), she builds three sides of a square, leaving the fourth side open. Then she builds correctly, out of three undivided spaghetti pieces, an angle $\wedge$, but she does not close it; then she replaces it by three sides of a quadrilateral. She repeats this procedure twice in spite of our admonitions to close the figure. However, with a quadrilateral whose long sides are of unequal length, Lis achieves closure by herself by bending one of the small sides (so that the figure becomes a semitrapezoid). This success is to be noted carefully, since every time she has to close three sides by a slanted line to make a triangular shape she simply does not get the idea: we have to start the figure for her and encourage her a great deal to continue! In spite of this half success of learning, in the following she only manages to construct figures like | | for a "park with three sides," of which she slants one side afterward.

Vin (4;2), whom we ask to "build shapes," constructs a sort of trapezoid (several), then open rectangles, one of which he closes by forming an acute angle. Then we ask for a roof, which he builds asymmetrically, completing it in various irregular ways. We then show him a model of a triangle to reproduce, which he does approximately. When asked to do another one, he ends up with a composition of nine elements whose upper portion is rectangular and lower consists of zigzag lines (including at least some pointed parts, which, on one occasion, he calls an *Indian tent*). Then we give him three pieces of spaghetti, asking him to build a "triangle" (the term had already been introduced): he immediately succeeds in building a square, looking for a way to complete the fourth side. Still, he agrees to label as triangles the models we propose to him. When asked to copy these in a drawing (he successfully completes squares and "rounds"), he achieves the remarkable result of a closed figure, which he completes with *a pointed thing*; but the body of this figure is a kind of ovoid, and the pointed thing a round cap!

Sti (5;6) shows very similar reactions, with a definite preference for quadrilaterals and the construction of an incomplete square (for a *park that's well closed*, using three equal pieces of spaghetti). With great difficulty and only after having watched the beginning of a demonstration by the experimenter, she finally brings two of the three sides together.

These observations show how a study on the development of possibilities should begin with an analysis of impossibility or, more precisely, an analysis of the factors that prevent the emergence of the possibilities initially expected by the experimenter! One might argue that there is nothing surprising about the difficulties these subjects have, since they simply have not yet acquired the presentative scheme of the triangle. However, this does not explain anything. The real question is how it is that subjects who are perfectly able to bend the rods to close a quadrilateral (see Lis, who makes explicit this intention, or Vin, with his trapeze shapes and trapezoids) cannot transfer this procedure to make a triangle and, although able to construct acute angles and "roofs," cannot complete these to make triangles. There must, therefore, be a systematic obstacle that prevents subjects from being open to this particular possibility. The obstacle takes the form of certain initial pseudonecessities that impose such limitations. This hypothesis is all the more acceptable because it is frequently verified in the history of science: even the great Aristotle saw only straight and circular movements as being possible, hence his erroneous representation of the pathways of projectiles (⌐↓). In the case of our three subjects, it is quite clear what the pseudonecessities are that constitute the barriers against the possibility of envisioning triangles: for these subjects, the only closed figures possible are quadrilaterals and circles. We have evidence of this in the subjects' free constructions, which are all of this type, and in Vin's marvelous graphic reproduction of a triangular model: perceiving it correctly at once as a closed figure equipped with a peak (an idea that runs counter to his pseudonecessary presentative schema), he represents it as an ovoid equipped with a cap to attenuate the contradiction. This compromise furnishes a first remarkable example of a frequent type of an emerging sensitivity to possibilities: the removal of a particular limitation (i.e., that only circles and quadrangles can be closed) while retaining as much of it as seems acceptable. The resulting figure and its "pointed tip" conserve here a curved and almost circular shape (even though Vin is perfectly capable of drawing squares and building acute angles, as in his "Indian tent").

Level I

Level IA presents itself as the extension of this new possibility—the closed form equipped with a tip. Here the procedures apply in reverse order to achieve the new goal. Unlike the younger subjects, who began by attempting to create a closed figure (which had to be circular or quadrilateral) and then tried laboriously to complete it by adding a tip (having difficulties with the oblique lines, etc.), these subjects begin by doing the tip, which they naturally call "the roof" (an already familiar presentative scheme), and only afterward will they work on closing the figure. At level IA, subjects consider this "roof" as immutable; they cannot conceive of altering its initial disposition while attempting to close it. The initiating function of this tip constitutes the most important innovation at this level, as compared with the opposite order of procedures observed in the younger subjects.

Yve (5;8) produces a right angle out of two pieces of spaghetti: *half of a square*, then adds a third, also at a right angle. "Can you do a triangle?" He constructs a roof with an extremely obtuse angle, adding a third element as a base, which is, however, too short to close the figure. "That's a triangle?" *Yes, because it's on the ground* [=the base] *and there are two across*. But he does not succeed in closing his figure. It never occurs to him to change the direction of one or the other side of the roof. The latter remains immutable. In the second task of part 2, he produces an acute angle: *That's half of the triangle, but it doesn't have a floor.* "You can cut them." he cuts the sticks but does not transform the pieces, so everything remains as it was. He finally succeeds in closing the figure by means of a fourth element that he adds from among the sticks not yet used. "Is that a triangle?" *Yes, a floor line and two across.* "And that [the fourth line]?" *That's to close the triangle.*

Cri (5;8) offers, in her spontaneous productions, some quadrilaterals and also *a house* with a closed triangle as a roof. *One can also make a letter*: she builds an *A* with a closed triangle as the upper element. But when asked to do a triangle, she produces a roof with a base too short for closure, even using two elements, and it does not occur to her to give a steeper inclination to one of the sides of her roof. "Can you do another one?" *I don't know how to do another triangle.* She keeps producing structures of the same type, unable to fill the *empty spaces*, that is, the gaps in her triangles. "Another one?" *No*, she declares categorically, *I cannot*. In the second task of part 2, she succeeds in closing the triangle but leaves some of the material unused. *So everything gets used up*, she produces a baseline that is far too long, extending on either side of the triangle. With the wire (part 3), she constructs a small tip and places two fingers so as to provide a baseline. Then she straightens out the rest of the wire. With three sticks, *a*, *d*, and *e* (part 4), which she chooses from among five, she succeeds in closing a triangle. To "make others," she tilts it so that the tip points downward, then to the left and to the right: *That's one down, one up, one that goes this way, and one goes that* [the other way]. But with *a*, *b*, and *c*, she regresses to open figures or ones whose sides are too long. When asked about "impossible triangles (*a*, *b*, *c*), she is not at all astonished, since she had already produced triangles that *have holes and that are too long*.

Jea (6;4) begins with eight approximately equilateral designs, six of which are closed on all three sides; two others have two sides unconnected, which he then closes with a fourth piece. He clearly concentrates mainly on the *point*, instead of the base and sides, *to finish the triangle*. Thus, he first directs the point *upward*, *then down*, *to the side*, and so on. Unlike Cri, he does not return to his initial triangle. In addition, his case is interesting in that he succeeds, while working with the sticks and trying to close a figure that remained open, in changing the position of one of the sides of the roof. He does this, not yet by modifying its inclination (as subjects do at level IB, which Jea anticipates), but by gradually shifting it from $\wedge$ to $\wedge$. Thus, the roof ceases to be immutable.

Level IB remains dominated by the procedure "the roof first," but followed by successful attempts to establish a relationship with the base and to close the figure. The important innovation at this level is the modification of the inclination of the roof, amounting to a change in angles (but still only by making it more acute, never more obtuse):

Eri's (5;11) first spontaneous construction is a rectangle. "And another shape?" *A triangle*. He builds it immediately as a closed equilateral, using three *a* pieces, after having hesitated between *c* and *d* as a base. With *b*, *a*, and *d*, he builds a roof *ab* and then notices that *d* is too short for a base. He encounters the same problem with other pieces. He solves the problem by elevating the base within the roof structure, which yields *A*—that is, a closed triangle but with useless extensions. When going on to part 2, he first constructs a roof and then spontaneously comes up with the idea of changing the angle: *Before it was like that* [about 60 degrees]; *now it's really tight*. When cutting the spaghetti to obtain three sides, he does not succeed at first in closing it. So he reduces the angle to facilitate closure. With three sticks in part 4, he begins as at level IA with an incomplete rectangular shape but immediately pulls the two long sides together to make an isosceles triangle. Then he reverses it so that *it drops down* or *goes up*. To demonstrate an impossible triangle, he chooses *a*, *d*, and *e*, saying that d *is medium sized*, a *is very big*, *and* e *very small*: that is, he selects the least equilateral.

Eus (6;2), with two pieces of spaghetti in part 2, spontaneously cuts off the ends; to achieve closure between the "roof" and the base, he slightly reduces the angle of the roof. For a second case, he repeats the same procedure and gradually succeeds in constructing an isosceles with a very acute angle on top. In part 3, he only makes an equilateral with one side protruding.

Ced (6;6), in part 1, begins with part of a quadrilateral, saying: *I wanted to make a square, but there isn't very much, so I'll do a triangle*. Then he makes an equilateral. "Can you do another one?" He immediately steepens the roof, building a very acute angle, even though the problem is not closing the figure but rather the base, as he says himself: *It's too long there*. In part 2, he also moves the angle around (but only in the direction of a steeper angle) of the roof-to-be, paying much less attention to the base (which still stands out). In part 3, he makes a very small tip above with the steel wire, then adjusts the remaining elements until he obtains a slender isosceles: *I try to do a really pointed one.* In part 4, he begins to give some attention to the base after a few rather unsuccessful productions, trying to eliminate protrusions. When using *e* and *d* as a roof and *c* as a base, he finds *c* too long. He works on the angle and then substitutes *b*, which is still longer than *c*. He finally achieves a good triangle, but with a very obtuse angle on top. These manipulations of the base forecast level II. However, when the experimenter proposes a similar triangle, but upside down (the tip pointed downward), Ced makes the following interesting comment: *That's not a triangle: one might say it's a sort of . . . . What's it called?* "A diamond?" *Yes, a diamond* [and, indeed, it is a half diamond!].

Sio (7;2), also after a great number of trials, succeeds in building a perfectly closed triangle with a very obtuse angle on top but doubts that it is really a triangle. "What is it?" *A triangle is a shape with three sides and three points: you can turn it any way you want, it makes a triangle.* But *this one, you can't turn it in all directions, it's too flat. . . . If I turn it, then it's no longer a triangle, then it's something else.* Although no longer accepting displacements, Sio still at first adjusts the base to the roof only by partial superpositions ($\overline{}$) internal to the figure.

Gro (6;3) and Rog (6;5), like the other subjects at this level, make significant progress toward closure, for the most part because of their newly acquired ability to narrow the angle of the roof. However, they do not yet succeed in eliminating protrusions at the ends, among other things because of their incapacity to widen angles.

Level IA is characterized by the new goal of building a figure that is both closed and has a tip, as a presentative schema, which is finally accepted after the difficulties described with less advanced subjects. This goal is described by Yve as a line "on the ground and . . . two across." A new procedure is also characteristic of this level: beginning with the roof and then trying to close it by means of the line on the "ground" serving as a base. But new problems arise because the roof, once built, becomes unalterable, for two reasons. One is almost affective: since the construction represents what was an obstacle before, and was difficult to overcome, it possesses a value to be preserved. The second is more serious: since the circle and the quadrilateral represent, up to this level, the only prototypical closed figures, subjects consider it important to conserve their internal symmetry and equivalence relations (radii or sides). Thus, the new candidate for the rank of a good closed figure has to respect these characteristics. This explains the systematic tendency to think of the triangle as equilateral, with a symmetrical roof and a horizontal base of about the same length as the two sides, with which they started. The immutability of the roof once constructed—the fact that the level IA subject never even considers the possibility of changing the slope of the sides—is another example of pseudonecessity, in continuity with and extension of the pseudonecessary squares or circles of our preliminary cases. The result is a particularly severe problem in constructing the base, in spite of its rather secondary role, which Jea describes somewhat condescendingly as the side "to finish the triangle": either it is made of elements that are too short, resulting in "empty spaces," which are deplored by Cri; or else it is too long and stands out at one or the other side of the roof, which the same Cri, rather sensibly, qualifies as "holes" that stand out. There is no need to repeat all the ups and downs of subjects' reactions, which we have described above in detail. One surprising accomplishment already observed at this level (IA) is the ability, seen in Cri and Jea, to orient the roof (called the "point") in different directions—upward, downward, or sideways. The explanation comes from the subjects Ced and Sio (at the end of level IB): a "true" triangle, which is seen as approximately an equilateral one (which may become an isosceles at level IB), is defined—like the circle and the square—as a figure that can be turned "any way you want" (unlike the obtuse roofs discovered at level IB). In this way, the triangle becomes a legitimate member of the set of acceptable good forms.

At level IB, subjects discover a new procedure that is designed to solve the problem of closure, which has been attempted but not solved up to then. (At level IA, subjects like Jea will go so far as to add a fourth side to "close the triangle," because they are unable to change the slopes: they remain quite unaware of the evident contradiction. To adjust the roof to the base, the level IB subjects, starting with Eri, finally succeed in narrowing the angle on the roof, reducing the distance between the two sides (but never trying to increase that distance, undoubtedly because that would amount to weakening the essential property of a "point": see Jea, who, already at level IA, frequently uses that term; as does Eri at level IB, who speaks of making it "really tight"; or Ced, who strives to "do a really pointed one"). This procedural advance results not only in facilitating closures but also in generalizing the presentative scheme of triangles by adding to the equilateral isosceles triangles, thus furnishing new goals; in short, enlarging the field of possibilities.

But these clear advances are still tempered by three kinds of limitations. The first is related to the pseudonecessities, the third to procedural problems, and the second to both at once. First, because of the pseudonecessary requirement of symmetry, the level IB subjects are incapable of identifying scalenes as triangles. Second, even when a triangle is symmetrical, if its roof is too obtuse it is not considered a "real" triangle because it is "too flat" (Sio), therefore not having an adequate "point," and when it is rotated it becomes "something else" (Sio)—that is, a half diamond (Ced). The third important limitation to be emphasized to appreciate the reversal in procedure that characterizes level II is the following: level IB subjects, even though they solve the problem of closure, do not succeed (because of their incapacity to widen the angle on the roof) in eliminating protrusions (Eus, etc.); when Ced begins to try to eliminate them, he approaches level II with his highly obtuse angle. Sio, the only one who rules out all protrusions, replaces these by partial superpositions within the same triangle. This amounts to an internal protrusion of one segment with respect to another one in cases where the base is built by means of several elements.

Level II

Subjects who are 7–8 years old or more succeed in eliminating altogether or in correcting these overextensions, because of a spectacular reversal of procedures: they establish the base before constructing the roof, instead of beginning with the latter. We are dealing here with the second reversal. The first characterized the change from the level of preliminary behaviors to level IA: to construct figures that are both closed and pointed, the subjects of level IA began by constructing a roof before attempting to close the triangle, whereas the subjects in the preliminary stage began by trying to build closed figures before adding a point to them. Similarly, to obtain figures that are at once closed and devoid of overextension, the subjects of level II begin with the base before adding a roof, whereas at level IB subjects achieved closure by decreasing the distance between the two sides of the roof but did not succeed at all in eliminating overextensions. Of course, it does not follow that the level II subjects succeed right away in predicting all possible overextensions: what they attempt to do is to avoid them after correcting for them, and thus to foresee precise junctures (without overextensions or gaps) of the three sides at once. Now, in beginning with the roof, only one of the three junctures can be assured (the one at the top), so that two others must be found (this is all the more difficult as, at level IB, subjects only succeed in narrowing, never in widening, the angle). On the other hand, by starting from the base subjects can establish two junctures at once—one at each end—so that only one additional juncture needs to be found by joining together the remaining ends of the two sides in any way feasible. This opens up a series of new possibilities that we shall analyze in the following, beginning with the intermediate cases—those who do not discover immediately the method base→roof. In many instances, the new procedures are not generalized to all problems presented to the subject.

Nat (7;0) presents a curious transitional case from level IB to II: she begins with an equilateral triangle, the roof first, then she uses a, b, and two c pieces to construct a partially composite base internal to the triangle (like Sio above). Next she constructs a narrow isosceles with a base that is too long, and right away she widens the angle on top, which is different from the reactions of level IB. After this, she begins a construction at the base. But the other two sides being rather long, she produces overextensions at the top from the two sides crossing, and then at both ends of the base. Only with corrections does she achieve the exact junctures. Then she builds another triangle (this time a rather flat one), beginning with the element that is by far the longest; then she builds a roof, which fails to connect to the end of the base, but she corrects this. She goes back to the roof-first procedure, correcting overextensions by widening angles. But her true above-level-IB performance is revealed in her spontaneous answer concerning impossible triangles (in part 4): she proposes *a* (17.5 cm), *d* (6.5 cm), and *e* (4 cm): *Like that there is a piece missing*; this she demonstrates by attaching *e* and *d* to each end of *a* and pointing out the gap.

Col (7;9) begins with constructions of roof→base, correcting these for overextensions and gaps. In one of these corrections she uses one side of the roof as a base, which results in a very obtuse angle. After an isosceles, roof first, we ask for a different one. *One can do a long piece down here* [points to the base] *and two small ones*, which she carries out, base first. For an impossible triangle she picks out, without the slightest hesitation, *a*, *d*, and *e* and demonstrates their nonclosure. "How should they be?" *Two the same size and a small one, and you squeeze them like this* [acute angle] *or two and a long one at the bottom and you spread them apart.*

Fab (7;2) in part 2 (two pieces of spaghetti) begins with the roof, leaving some pieces unused, then uses a whole spaghetti piece as a base and cuts the other one into two unequal pieces to construct the sides: *I put a long one here* [base] *and I broke one in two and I made a roof.* With a single spaghetti piece, which she cuts in three, she builds a scalene with a very obtuse angle on top. In part 4, she keeps fitting two sides to a single base, trial after trial.

Arc (7;8) works with the five sticks, trial and error, without success. With three sticks, he places the longest one as a base and the two other ones as sides at each end, and he joins these to produce a scalene: *First I did that* [the base], *then the others.* "And another one?" He substitutes new sticks for the sides of the previous roof, joining them to the same base. He then generalizes the procedure base→roof, using a very short stick as a base (*e*) and fitting a tall, pointed roof (*a* and *b*); then he repeats the procedure with shorter sticks on each side (*c* and *d* on base *e*). For an impossible triangle, he spontaneously designates *a*, *e*, and *d*: *You can't do anything with those*, demonstrating this at both ends of the base. Then we ask him to draw and he provides eight different ones, but all with a horizontal base as the first element. The first and the sixth are isosceles, and the others are scalenes with varied angles: "What is a triangle?" *It's a bar on the bottom* [base] *and a thing like this* [indicates a roof].

Ana (8;3) begins with drawings, which are interesting in that, even though they always come with the roof first, they vary in the size of the angle on top. Later the various triangles get positioned in different ways. In part 4, she immediately lays down the base, which is either *a* alone or *c*+*e*, fitting to it the sides of the roof.

Myr (8;3) uses trial and error in part 2 with one or two spaghetti pieces, which she cuts. Soon she spontaneously adopts the method base→roof. For an impossible triangle, she immediately lays down *e* and *c* horizontally over *b* to show that *you cannot close it*.

We see the extent to which the new procedure of beginning with the base breeds new possibilities that manifest themselves as new goals and as extensions of existing presentative schemes, accompanied by a new freedom from pseudonecessities — including symmetries and horizontal bases. As soon as subjects see, when beginning from the two ends of the base, that one can erect sides of any length whatever provided their sum exceeds the length of the base (this ability is clearly demonstrated by the subjects on the impossible triangle task), all shapes become acceptable, scalenes as well as symmetrical ones, roofs with very obtuse as well as very acute angles. (In contrast, subjects like Ced and Sio at level IB systematically refuse to widen the angle at the top, agreeing only to make it narrower.) In addition, Arc and others discover the new possibility of changing the size of angles and sides while conserving the base.

How does this new procedure of starting with the base get elaborated? Our observations appear to confirm what we predicted above: instead of simply proceeding by successive corrections and paying more heed to closure than to overextensions, these subjects sooner or later — or sometimes immediately — become concerned with the three points of juncture simultaneously; that is, they decide to begin with the base. This idea may arise in various ways. Some subjects, like Nat, in attempting to correct overextensions, widen the angle on top in a way that corresponds to the earlier narrowing of the angle that was the only possible procedure at level IB. In this case, when the base thus becomes correct, subjects get the idea of starting with a similar base. In Col's case, similarly, the corrections made on the roof suggest the possibility of using one side as a base, followed again by a widening of the top angle. In Fab and Myr, the contrast between a whole and the broken spaghetti facilitates the start with the base; in Arc it is the choice of the longest one (soon generalized to the opposite: that is, to narrow isosceles triangles as opposed to the flattened scalenes). For Ana, it is the variety of shapes she draws as possible, from very narrow isosceles to extremely flat scalenes (without considering the fact that connections are relatively easy to make on the drawing task) that gives her the idea in part 4 to begin with a long base. Let us recall that the very flat triangles are not considered as "real" triangles at level IB. In contrast, at level II, the widening of the upper angle and the extension of the base are the actions that most often lead subjects to begin with the latter.

The following conclusions can be drawn concerning the transition from level IA to level II and the new possibilities associated with this transition. At level IA the roof, once constructed, remains immutable because it represents the essence of a triangle, which is to have a point. At level IB it becomes possible to narrow the angle but not yet to widen it because a narrow roof remains a part of the immutable roof required at level IA, whereas a wider roof becomes something different. At level II this limitation disappears at once because a variation in one direction comes to entail a reciprocal one in the other (symmetry) and because the increasing concern with precise junctures brings about the freedom to change the shape of the roof. As for the base, at level IA it plays a totally secondary, complementary role, and when it is too short it is still accepted as a base, or it may be completed by a fourth element to "close the triangle" (Yve). At level IB its closing function becomes more precise, and subjects give more attention to it. This is related to the possibility of narrowing the roof if necessary. Still, some overextensions persist. At level II, however, these are carefully eliminated, as are the gaps. This in turn leads to the procedure of establishing the base first, which guarantees the completion of the three junctures; these need not be imagined in advance, since two of them are given by the two ends of the base and the third (the point of the roof) can easily be obtained by simply joining the two sides (except for Nat, who begins by crossing the two). As for possibilities, they are generated in analogical succession at level IA, whereas retroactive corrections become frequent at level IB. The main characteristic of level II is then the development of anticipatory behaviors, which allow subjects to discern, after a few trials, the advantages and disadvantages of choosing such and such an element and to strive to consider the three junctures simultaneously. In this way, the goal to be reached comes to be represented in more precise, clearer presentative schemes.

Concerning the presentative schemes to which the procedures lead, we note a fairly simple extension of the field of possibilities. A form of pseudonecessity resulting from an analogy with circular or quadrilateral figures initially dictates the primacy of equilateral triangles. In level IB there is a substantial increase in narrow isosceles triangles, which occurred occasionally at level IA, facilitated by the new possibility available to subjects of narrowing the top angle; flat isosceles and especially scalenes, however, are rigorously ruled out at that level (even at 7;2 years, Sio still says that a scalene "is not a triangle," because the two sides that form the roof must be the same length). Finally, at level II, all shapes including the scalenes erected on a base are valid, and the base does not even necessarily have to be horizontal.

Level III

At level II, the construction of triangles seems to reach its final development. However, there are still some limitations as to the generality—the number of imaginable possibilities and the indeterminate nature of the orientations and lengths of the side that can serve as bases but with all sides being equivalent to each other. First, a few observations:

Mar (10;9), in part 1, constructs an equilateral and then an inclined scalene with a narrow horizontal base, which she modifies to give it a right angle, slanting the base. She goes on to an equilateral, conserving the right angle. Then she draws many different kinds of shapes, using as a base any element whatever. For the impossible triangle she correctly chooses *e*, *a*, and *d*, placing *d+e* horizontally against *a* and saying that they *should be the same length as the stick* [*a*]. "And with those [*b*, *c*, and *e*]?" She measures them as before and concludes that $c+e<b$. *Yes, that's alright.*

Oli (11;4) in part 2 takes measurements before cutting the spaghetti *to know if I could get a tip at the end.* For the impossible triangle he also lines up *d* and *e* against *a* to give a demonstration.

Lyd (12;2), after having done eight very different drawings, says: *You'll make me completely run out of triangle!* When asked to compare two figures that only differ in height, she adds: *So, to continue to infinity you would have smaller and smaller triangles* [=flatter]; similarly, in increasing the height *one can go on and on. . . .* "How many times?" *You can't tell because they can all be very different. For example, I can do that one and then the same one again, but adding one-tenth of a millimeter: it's always different.* After that she classifies the triangles according to whether three sides are equal, or two sides, or *that one has nothing — well — none of the sides are equal*, also according to whether the triangle constitutes half of a square or a rectangle. "Up until now, you have only talked about the sides." *They can't be done without angles.* "With three sides, one necessarily obtains a triangle?" *In my view, one could do something else* [=side by side: she draws them — —]. *That makes a flat — what do you call it — a null angle.*

As usual, we find here the culmination of the development of possibilities when they take the form of "any way whatever" in intension (as when Mar imagines any possible shape and relativizes the notion of baseline) and of infinity in extension (as manifest in Lyd's statements). Two specific acquisitions must be noted: the first is the restricted number of "families" of possible triangles (equilaterals, etc.), each of which includes an infinity of variations in size and shapes (such as the scalene, with its infinitely many degrees of flattening being described as "smaller and smaller" triangles). The second acquisition, amazingly spontaneous, is the absolute limit to the infinitely many variations in the size of an angle, the "flat" or "null angle."

This research furnishes a nice illustration of the growth of possibilities concerning procedural and presentative schemes in alternation. At first (preliminary cases), the problem is simply to conceive of the goal in order to find the means to realize it, and the presentative scheme of a figure equipped with a tip is not easy to understand as long as the closed figures are only circular or quadrilateral. Once the goal is conceptualized, the procedures of level IA (roof first, but immutable) leave many problems of closure and overextension unresolved: procedural progress at this level consists, then, in the ability to narrow the angles and to limit the initial pseudonecessity of equilateral triangles up to the presentative scheme of the isosceles. There remains still the pseudonecessity of symmetry and the pseudoimpossibility of overly flattened isosceles triangles. From here, the double procedural innovation of level II — widening of the angles and building the base first — leads to the remarkable presentative extension of the inclusion of scalene triangles, the way to the generalizations of level III.

But two additional comments are called for. The first has to do with the particular complexity of level II: the method of building the base first, in fact, presupposes a certain amount of presentative anticipation of junctures without overextensions — that is, of the goal that provokes the procedural invention of widening angles and of the role of the base. In turn, these new means (as often happens because of the asymmetry: means→end, new means→broadening of the goal) lead to the presentative innovation of scalenes (not envisioned before the invention of the new procedures). The second comment concerns the rather surprising convergence of the results obtained by means of the drawings and the material constructions, whereas one might expect that conceptual understanding would play a greater part in the goals proposed in the drawings. In fact, one finds the initial nonclosures and overextensions as well as the sequence of roof first — base first in the drawings as much as in the other tasks, even though the relativization of the position of the base is more rapid in the drawing task.

Finally, in a semistructured study like this one (problem solving), the new possibilities do not result simply from free combinations but are associated with procedures designed to correct certain imperfections; in other words, they compensate for certain disturbances within a process of successive equilibrations: to repair nonclosures at level IB and overextensions at level II. In addition, in other situations, subjects must liberate themselves from certain limitations, as in the transition between the preliminary cases to those of level IA, where subjects seek to reconcile the point with closure; or, in quite a different sense, in the change from the finiteness of level II to the infinity characteristic of level III. The question of whether these limitations, which result from pseudonecessities or from deficiencies in intrinsic variations, constitute some kind of virtual disturbances, which the new possibilities then compensate for, has already been discussed at the end of chapter 9.

13

Construction with a Compass

with C. Voelin and E. Rappe-du-Cher

The construction of triangles with sticks suggested to us that of curvilinear shapes by means of a compass. The disadvantage of this task is, of course, that the compass is completely unfamiliar to the youngest children, whereas children of a certain age use it in school. Still we may analyze the emergence of possibilities, since (as we shall see) these are independent of the use made of it in teaching and in children's schoolwork. In fact, what interests us here is not only how subjects understand the compass, but also the way they decompose and recompose the circle and the curvilinear figures that may result from these activities. Just as, in the triangle task, the successive emergence of new possibilities leads from the equilateral to the isosceles and, finally, the scalene, in correspondence with the procedures used, the circle, in spite of appearances, also gives rise to quite different possibilities, depending on whether it is conceptualized in a purely figurative fashion or in relation to the center and the radii: hence its decomposition into various arcs may lead to recompositions as quarters of the moon, as lenses, and so forth. We want to understand the factors that make these constructions and their development possible.

We give subjects various types of compasses (a pencil compass = a pencil enclosed in a metal frame; a lead compass = a metal compass), a pencil, and paper. We ask subjects what they can do with "that," and then what "other things" they can do. When a child does not find any more possibilities, we present four slates covered with complex designs of compasses (intersections, nesting, crisscrossings of curved lines, etc.); these are only presented for a short duration, which does not permit copying. The only purpose is to make the child aware that there are still many other combinations possible. At the end of the interview, we suggest (if the subject has not mentioned it) that it is possible to use the compass to calculate distances.

Level I

The initial reactions are of interest because they show the subjects' failure to comprehend the relations between the point of the compass and the circle that the pencil draws around this center:

Kar (3;5) knows, of course, nothing of compasses. He can only perceive it as a pencil in a metal frame, *so it doesn't break.* When we show him how to draw a circle, he follows the procedure attentively. Then having brought the point and the pencil together, he moves them in parallel, joining their ends. He obtains a small rectangle, which he calls *a round;* thereafter he prefers to do some better ones using only the pencil.

Isa (4;0) cannot see the use of the *little pin* either, and she draws nothing in particular with the pencil. We show her how to trace the arc of a circle: she completes it, using only the pencil, and draws a sun. We do it again and she closes the arc to a half-moon. We draw two circles intersecting; this time she tries to imitate, fixating the point and correctly making the pencil rotate, producing three-quarters of a circle. To complete it, she places the point at a distance of 1 cm away from the initial center. The result is an arc starting at the end of the first one and then turning toward the center. "Is that a round?" *Almost.* She evidently does not see any relation between the center and the circumference.

Guy (4;5) already knows that the compass serves *to draw circles.* "How did you find out?" *I always know everything.* "And what is that?" *A pin.* "How is it used?" *It's for making a round.* He takes the compass, makes a hole with the point, then draws a big circle with the pencil alone without paying attention to the point or the hole. We ask for others, but he still makes no effort to keep the point in place when he draws the round. We give a demonstration: *Me, I don't do it like you.* "How did I do it?" *You first made a hole and then a circle, a very little one.*

Val (4;10), shows the same reactions. After a round drawn with the pencil: "Now, can you do it with the pencil part and the point?" *I'll do a square, and after, I'll do the point.*

Nal (5;2), comparing her rounds with those we drew with the compasses: "Is there a difference?" *Yes, that one* [compass] *is round everywhere, it's more round.* "Why?" *Because that makes it more round.*

Gre (5;6): *My mom has taught me to make a round with that.* And, in fact, he draws using the compasses correctly. When asked to describe his actions he only says about the point, which has remained in place: *I don't need that. I did it with the pencil* [of the compass]. "Which works better, that [the compasses] or that [the free pencil]? *That one* [the compasses], *because you can do like this* [he correctly repeats the action]. *That* [the point], *that isn't used for anything, so we do the round like that* [with the pencil]. "When you drew the square [which he had done with the pencil of the compasses], what did the point do?" *Well, nothing, it stayed in the same place, in the middle* [a complete illusion]. "And when you draw the rounds, what does it do?" *Nothing at all.* "Did you place it there [in the middle]?" *No, by itself.* "You didn't do it on purpose?" *Oh, no.* "Is it better to have it in the middle or could it be anyplace?" *I'd rather have it there* [on the circumference], *because if it were there* [center] *one couldn't draw.*

These reactions show that the formation of possibilities does not, in this particular case, result from subjects' sensorimotor behaviors (that is, their abilities to manipulate the compasses) but rather from the relations they are able (or unable) to establish in the course of their actions. These behaviors and the use subjects make of the compasses are very different from one subject to the next (and even more so than we can cite in detail). The youngest subjects do not perceive the compasses as a unified object and use the point alone to have fun making holes and stripes (like Kar with his rectangle), whereas the more advanced subjects consider the hole as a necessary element, since there is a point and the compasses form a whole. This view is evident, for example, in Val's reaction, who plans to do a square, adding, "After, I'll do the point." Some subjects have never seen compasses, whereas Guy knows that they are used "to draw circles," and Gre even knows how to use them correctly. But in spite of this great variability in behavior, the relations subjects establish between goals and means before or after they can see the results of their actions are the same for all subjects and can be described as follows:

(1) A circle is simply a curved shape. Its main characteristics are essentially figurative and have to do with the circumference or the perimeter, which has to be "round everywhere" (Nal), hence the advantage of the compasses, which can draw "more round" than other pencils. (2) The figurative circle has in itself neither center nor equal radii leading from it to the circumference (see the first notions of equal distances described in chapter 11). (3) Even if the point and the hole are seen as being located in the "middle" (Gre), that does "nothing at all," and the "little pin" (Isa) got there "by itself," as Gre says; but that is wrong because it would be better, he adds, on the circumference so that it would not interfere with the drawing of the circle. As for Isa, the circle she begins is not at all seen in relation to the point; to complete it, she positions the point elsewhere, surprised that she thus obtains only "almost" a round. Guy makes a hole and then draws a circle with the pencil of the compass without referring in any way to the point. When he is shown the procedure to be followed, he interprets it as: "You first made a hole and then . . . a little circle." Val and Gre believe that the square also needs a hole.

Whether or not they know compasses, whether or not they succeed in using them correctly, subjects at this level fail to abstract the relationships that their manipulations seem to imply and that this manipulation should help to conceptualize. Thus, these kinds of possibilities are clearly not predetermined, neither in the object nor even in the subjects' partial successes. Their formation will require, as we have seen with the triangle (chapter 12), the development of processes like decomposition and recomposition that confer new meanings to observable phenomena, which until then were not powerful enough to develop in the direction of intrinsic variations and deducible co-possibilities.

Level II

Relational possibilities of this kind appear first at 7–8 years of age: Lau (7;2) knows that compasses serve to "make rounds" and she is willing to try it, with some hesitation: *I can't do it. It's not going very well*; but, in fact, she succeeds in drawing a 12-cm circle with only a 2-cm gap. She explains: *You put the point in the middle, and then you turn it.* Following this, she draws another circle of about 5 cm, and we ask her to do another just like that one. It does not occur to her to measure the radius: *No, it is bigger. . . . Perhaps if I put one on top* [she reinserts the point exactly in the center of her previous circle and retraces the circumference]. "Where did you put the point that writes?" *On the border of the round.* "And the metal point?" *In the middle.* "Can one do other things than circles? *A triangle.* She traces the arc of a circle with the compasses, then draws the two other sides with the pencil. "Is it perfect?" *Not quite. It's not made for that.* "Are there compasses for making squares?" *No!!* [energetically] "Or for ovals?" *I don't know.* "And with several circles, one can make shapes?" *Yes.* She traces a full circle and three partial ones (three-quarters of the circumference adjoining it). *A flower!* She then offers two more circles with an intersection and two crossed arcs.

Tan (7;0): *One has to push on that* [the point] *and then turn it.* After a success, she adds, spontaneously: *One can make big ones and little ones with it*, and she varies the gap between the points. But she does not see other patterns, even though she agrees that there may be others possible. *Perhaps one can.* But when we ask for two equal circles made with two different compasses, she succeeds by adjusting the compasses: *I found the right way.* Furthermore, after a brief glance at the designs we show her, she constructs all sorts of intersecting patterns, then comes up with a very original project: three arcs of a circle, with adjustments of the compass and completed by a free drawing of notches, between two of which: *a clover leaf.*

Nat (8;0) believes that she has already seen a compass and that *one can trace rounds with it*, but she does not know how to use it. She tries and traces an arc of a circle, then to complete the circle she poses the point on the paper *to finish it.* In doing so, she discovers that the point *helps us to turn. If the point wasn't there, it would be impossible to trace* [the circle], *to make it very round.* "Why?" *One has to keep the same distance. One has to keep the point at the same length—it has to stay the same, the same length* [she points to the compass and indicates how the gap has to stay constant]. *You set it when you want to start and it stays like that in the middle*. In fact, Nat abstracts here not only the notion of the center but also that of the equality of the radii, which she specifies as follows: *One can decide on a length, one can set it* [the compass], *then one puts it in the middle and keeps the same length* [i.e., the radius]. Squares and triangles cannot be done *because one has to turn the pencil like that*. The designs, which she looks at for a moment, inspire her to do concentric circles only.

Gen (8;3) similarly discovers the relation of center to radius when we ask him to construct a circle the same size as another circle (15 cm in diameter) drawn on a cardboard somewhat removed from the table. Gen successively adapts the following three means: (1) He spreads the two arms of the compass to encompass the model circle, which, of course, requires adjustments depending on the position; (2) he places the two arms of the compass — in vertical position — over any two locations on the circumference, but not over the diameter; (3) *I put the point in the middle* and the pencil over the circumference, thus taking a measure of the radius. He checks and verifies that the distance remains the same at the opposite end, therefore he succeeds in reproducing the model. To do an oval, he says that *one needs to measure*. . . . "Can one measure it with a compass?" *Yes, one can measure*. When we ask him to reproduce a rectangle, he begins by placing the point in the middle, which would permit the construction of a *circle of the same size*; then he measures the width of the rectangle but soon concludes: *Yes, but one has to do it twice*, and he takes the measure of the length as well. Having briefly looked at the complex designs, he only produces a circle surrounded by semicircles.

Cri (8;10): Her reactions are interesting with regard to measuring. When we ask her to reproduce a kind of a square, she says: *No, one can only reproduce round shapes*. . . . *I would need a ruler*. Then she places the compass to measure height and says: *Oh yes! I think one can use the compass as a ruler. So one can take measures*. . . .

If one compares Nat, who first fails to construct a circle correctly but in the end discovers the invariance of the radii ("One has to keep the same distance"), with Gre, who, at level I, builds circles without hesitating but does not even have the notion of a center, one cannot help being impressed by the way new possibilities emerge at level II. These possibilities are unknown to subjects at level I, even though some of their behaviors appear to imply their availability (but only apparently, and only from the point of view of the observer). The novelty in question is the discovery of the notion of the center of rotation, the "middle" (Lau, Nat, etc.); that of the gap or distance between the points of the compass (Tan); that of the equality of the radii (Nat and Gen); and the use of the compass as a measuring instrument (Gen and Cri). Once the construction of a circle is understood, other possibilities are added, such as partial circles (arcs), combinations, and intersections, which Lau finds even before being shown our designs. Other subjects find them afterward, but invent their own.

The specific character of the new possibilities appearing at level II is that they concern not free compositions or actions (except in the case of the final variations) nor optimalizations in specific performances (since circles can already be achieved at level I), but rather a change in interpretation in the direction of intrinsic variations that are interrelated by necessary links. Thus, we have to do here with deducible possibilities that develop when subjects discover that a center of rotation and a constant distance between the points of the compass—corresponding to the length of the radii, which are equal to one another—are the conditions for the construction of circles and that a circle is not simply a figural object with a perimeter "round everywhere" (as Nal said at level I). In other words, these new possibilities derive from the fact that the circumference is no longer thought of as a simple figure, but as an outcome. The problem is then to establish the conditions and effects of varying these conditions (as when Tan varies the gap or Gen tries out different positions with the compass for the purpose of measurement). It may be argued that in these cases of deducible possibilities there are no more inventions, but only a becoming conscious of predetermined implications. However, we claim that in every domain, including higher mathematics, an implication exists only after it has been constructed: when Cantor discovered that the correspondence between the series 1, 2, 3 . . . ; 2, 4, 6 . . . ; implies the existence of the transfinite cardinal aleph-null, which does not belong to either of these series but expresses the property common to both (i.e., the "power" of enumeration), this implication only existed after it had been constructed and only became "necessary" as a result of the operations of establishing correspondences, which rendered it possible. Only then could the various possibilities become related to one another by necessary links.

Level III

Related to the preceding level by various intermediate cases, the final level is characterized by the possibility of constructing all combinations of curvilinear elements and the impossibility of obtaining straight lines:

Pac (10;0), after drawing a circle, constructs quarter moons of increasing sizes, then a lens, and insinuates an oval by combining the curves. He reproduces from memory the symbol of the Olympic games and finally produces an irregular agglomeration within an approximately circular frame, but supplied with four protrusions and containing lenses, crescents, and so on, without a particular pattern. As for "impossible" forms, they are only rectilinear *because if one wanted to draw straight lines, one would have to turn after having placed the point.*

Adi (10;11): *One can draw anything, except squares.*

Ser (11;0) offers a series of close, concentric circles, and this gives him the idea of a snail, which he draws by making the gap *smaller and smaller*. He does not dismiss the possibility of a triangle, but makes it curvilinear: *That's like a shield*. "And in three dimensions?" He makes a quadrilateral, also with somewhat curved lines, which he prolongs to create a three-dimensional effect, a kind of tube with ridges. *That's a kind of rounded square*; then he creates multiple circles intersecting in irregular ways: *One should stop after a certain number, but I don't know how many*.

Ser (11;6), to do "something that is not round," constructs an elegant sinusoid.

Vin (11;7): *Almost everything is possible except a straight line*, but there may be *completely illogical curves*. He gives as an example a figure resembling a scorpion with wings and many tails but without symmetrical lateral parts, one side being larger than the other. Further, he constructs beautiful spirals leading upward, a snail on a plane, and so on.

Bel (12;0): *I think one can do anything with compasses, except for very straight lines*.

These reactions from subjects who use compasses in their geometry courses show that the problem we pose has nothing to do with the use they are put to in school teaching. Rather, it consists essentially in drawing all possible forms with the use of this instrument. We also observe in this task that subjects, after first having produced a few correct shapes, do not hesitate to engage in possibilities of unlimited extension, including random or irregular shapes — even to what Vin designates as "completely illogical curves." On the other hand, even though all subjects unanimously exclude the possibility of straight lines, some of them (we only cite Ser [11;0] as an example among others) take pleasure in showing that even triangles and squares may be obtained if their sides are slightly curvilinear (by spreading the arms of the compass as far apart as possible). These subjects also furnish recurrent variations, such as the concentric circles of Ser and their transformations into spirals by continuous modification of the width of the compass.

The reactions of level III are thus similar to those we find for this level in almost all our studies, even though we are dealing here with a very particular instrument (as opposed to, say, rods to be combined), which provides a limited scope of construction — i.e., those involving curvilinear forms (aside from the length measures already acquired at level II). The possibilities finally attained in this specific domain present the usual two characteristics: the "any which way" in intension ("One can draw anything, except squares," says Adi, even to the "completely illogical" of Vin); and an unlimited extension ("One can do anything," says Bel; only Ser [11;0] concedes a numerical limit, which he is unable to specify).

Comparing, finally, the construction of these curvilinear forms to those of triangles, one finds that in both cases there is variation from one level to the next in the presentative schema of the goal to be reached and, thus, of the figure to be obtained. These changes correspond closely to variations in procedures. The circle is nothing but a figurative "round" shape at level I, just as the triangle corresponding to the procedure "roof first" is nothing but a shape with a pointed tip that has to be closed. In contrast, when subjects understand the role of the center and of the gap between the arms of the compass, they become able to decompose and recompose radii and circumference deductively; similarly, in the case of the triangle, the strategy "base first" leads to anticipated closures and to generalization of the figure in the form of scalenes in addition to the symmetrical forms. Finally, at level III, there is relativity of the base of the triangle, hence an infinity of possible triangles, just as the "good forms" of the curvilinear type come to be members of the indefinite set of any curvilinear forms whatever—constrained, however, by the relation $[A > (B + C)]$ in the case of the triangle and by the impossibility of straight lines in the case of the compasses.

Conclusions

I

The first question we wish to discuss (even though it has already been touched upon in several chapters) concerns the relation between the evolution of possibilities, which is seen to be very regular and general, and the sequence of levels of operational thought. This relationship is so direct that we were able to make use of the same stages to describe the development of both: to the preoperational level I there correspond possibilities generated by successive analogies; at level IIA, at the onset of concrete operations, we find the formation of concrete co-possibilities; at level IIB (the level of equilibrium for concrete operations) there are the co-possibilities, which we have simply labeled *abstract*, but only in the sense that they are generalized to cases other than those actually realized; finally, at level III of the hypothetico-deductive operations appear the indeterminate co-possibilities of "any . . . whatever," unlimited in number. Thus, we find a very striking parallelism, but the question remains as to how to explain it and, particularly, which of the two developments stimulates the other and by what mechanism.

From the point of view of operations, level I is characterized by the absence of reversibility, of recursivity, etc. — in short, by the absence of systematic inferences and closures. By analyzing the manner in which possibilities are generated (i.e., by successive analogies that are typical of this level), we clearly see the reasons for these shortcomings. First, analogy is a combination of major similarities with minor differences, but without transitivity in the way each follows upon the other: B can be analogous to A with respect to a particular similarity x, and C to D with respect to another one, y, without C necessarily being analogous to A. Obviously, the number of ways one possibility is generated from the preceding one in this nontransitive fashion is far greater than would be the case for implicitly transitive modes of succession. Second, one and the same goal can

145

be attained by several possible means or procedures and a given procedure can inspire new goals in addition to the initial goals; consequently, the initial system is abandoned. Thus we see that there is an internal asymmetry between the sets of possibilities and operational structures: the former are, for the reason just given, much more numerous than the latter and also than the preoperational half structures (nonfigurative collections, etc.). A third aspect, which was analyzed in chapter 8, is given by the overdeterminations and overcompositions as they generate possibilities, as opposed to operational compositions, which are well delimited within closed systems.

The result of these various facts is twofold: the relations composed as actualizable possibilities are too heterogeneous and the mode of their composition (successive analogy) is too simple to permit the formation of even very simple operations with their well-delimited and well-regulated structures. But should one then attribute the absence or relatively late appearance of operations to the deficient or slow-developing possibilities, or, inversely, is the primitive nature of the possibilities caused by the absence of operations that could generate them? The problem, formulated in this way, is unsolvable unless one invokes an interaction in a negative mode, which should be described in terms of mutual restrictions or disturbances. But there is also a positive aspect that can help us to understand the relations developing between the domain of possibilities and that of operations: even at level I, the emergence of possibilities bears witness to an accommodating activity, choice behavior, sequential productions of various kinds, regulations, and so on; all these constitute the raw material for the development of the emerging operations. At the very least, the possibilities found at level I constitute a general framework within which procedures are progressively refined up to the concrete co-possibilities characteristic of level IIA. When this happens, we can clearly see and determine the relations between the novel forms of possibilities and operations.

But at first sight the situation seems just as ambiguous at level IIA as at the preceding one: the synchronism between the constitution of inferential co-possibilities and of operations appears so complete that one can only discern interactions between two associated developmental processes. In fact, it appears that all one can do is appeal again to a common mechanism—that of equilibration. The latter, as we have seen, is complex and can take multiple forms. So it remains for us to analyze the relative contributions of the factors involved. This will lead us back to our original problem of the relations between the general procedures generating co-possibilities and the more restricted and regulated ones that characterize operations and the development of their structures. Because operational compositions are of a necessary nature, whereas co-possibilities have a much wider range, it would be difficult to argue that necessity could engender the empirical data. The question becomes simpler when formulated in the opposite way: under which conditions does the subject, in possession of this extended framework, come to develop the specific forms of possibilities that are capable of closure—that is, the operational transformations?

The answer is undoubtedly that the operations result not from the co-possibilities per se, with their diversified content and their essentially analogical nature, but rather from the inferential act, which generates them as being simultaneously co-possible. This act is of a higher order than simple sequential, linear associations, and it is apt to produce the reflective abstractions and completive generalizations that can lead to the development of operations. Three processes appear to be involved in this development.

In the first, anticipating co-possibilities instead of proceeding in simple, successive, and stepwise fashion, multiple and simultaneous connections come into play. These connections, as diversified as they are in content, can yield general, regulatory forms: that of union as a function of similarities and differences, which is the starting point for the emergence of classes; that of ordination as a function of quantitative variations, constituting the principle of seriation. This does not mean that classification and seriation derive from co-possibilities in content, even though, exceptionally, these may be partially classified or seriated. It means, however, that the very act of anticipating several possibilities at the same time may become, inasmuch as it involves the establishment of relationships, the source of connections that can be generalized and regulated and that, in this way, appear in the form of classes and series.

But to achieve this, a second condition has to be met: the system of similarities and differences, the only one involved in the formation of possibilities, has to be completed by a system of affirmations and negations that are indispensable to operations. It is true that each difference partly implies negation, but what counts in the genesis of possibilities is the creation of a new variation, and this innovation is an acquisition of positive valence. In contrast, in the genesis of classes and seriations, differences must be associated with explicit partial negations such that if A', subclass of B, differs from A, then $A' = B$ not A, or $A' = B - A$. Similarly, in seriation, a positive change must be accompanied by changes in the opposite direction. We have studied elsewhere the difficult regulation of these negative factors.* Their equilibration with the positive ones is a condition sine qua non for the transition of co-possibilities to operations.

A third condition is the establishment of a connection between possibility and necessity ('X is necessary' implies that not-X is impossible or even intrinsically contradictory): in other words, the change from co-possibilities, which only concern extrinsic variations (free choice between empirical properties, which, however, can be anticipated simultaneously), to intrinsic variations that are considered co-possible because of deduced connections (an example is given in level II of chapter 10). Thus, as soon as co-possibilities get constituted, the transition

---

*See *Experiments in Contradiction* (Chicago: University of Chicago Press, 1980).

from one possibility to another tends to become inferential and to lead, if the data are suitable, to the development of a deductive mechanism — necessity.

The formation of concrete operations thus proceeds within a larger developmental process that determines it. But this result is mediated by reflective abstractions and more advanced regulations in the mechanism generating possibilities. These relationships are even more evident at level IIB with its abstract co-possibilities since, beginning to go beyond the domain of actualization, the subjects deduce the possibilities as such, forming virtual classes or seriations of which the individual terms realized are only exemplars or representatives.

One might object that, if operations derive from the activities that generate possibilities, that means that operations from the moment they come into being determine the evolution of possibilities. At first sight, this hypothesis seems confirmed by the transition from level II to level III, where the indeterminate, unlimited possibilities become completely deducible, based on recursive mechanisms that go far beyond any kind of empirical control. This final victory of intrinsic over extrinsic variations certainly attests to the decisive role that operations come to play. But would it have come about in the absence of the prior, specific advances in the development of possibilities as such? To answer this question, we have to consider these developments within the context of the relationships developing with age between possibility, reality, and necessity.

II

As we already pointed out in the introduction and as substantiated in most of the chapters, the young subject does not begin by considering reality only, constituted by pure observables, and later complete this by constructing possibilites and necessary relations. Rather, the ontological status of the initial state is one of nondifferentiation: reality as perceived or manipulated appears as being necessarily as it is so that it represents the only possibility, except for occasional variations that are accepted as realizable because they have already been observed and are, therefore, part of a particular sector of the same nondifferentiated reality. It would be superfluous to repeat here what was described in several places above concerning pseudonecessities. We only wish to recall two essential points: First, the formation of possibilities does not proceed by simple free associations but consists rather in real *openings* requiring a liberation from limitations and obstacles of varying strength. Second, these limitations result from the fact that within this initial nondifferentiation, reality, possibility, and necessity (genuine, not pseudonecessity) block one another's development — that is, each hinders the development of the other two complementary modalities. If this is true, to arrive at a harmonious integration into a coherent system (which is an essential condition for the formation of operational structures) the three must become differentiated, following their own respective developmental course distinct and independent of the others.

To understand these initial blockings and disturbances we first need to recall that only reality by itself, composed of known or still unknown objects and events, exists independently of the subject, even though it becomes knowable only under the condition that it gets assimilated and interpreted by the subject. In contrast, possibility and necessity are the products of subjects' activities. Where possibility is concerned, this is clearly true for free combinations of actions; but even for virtual, physical possibilities we have seen in chapters 6 and 7 that they remain relative to subjects' inferences. As for necessity, because relationships between "real" events can only be general to a greater or lesser extent, their necessity always remains part of the models that subjects construct deductively, hence subordinated to the necessary laws pertaining to these deductions themselves.

Given these considerations, it is evident that the initial lack of differentiation results essentially from an insufficiency of subjects' activities concerning possibilities and necessity; what they consider as reality, in turn, comprises illegitimate incursions into the domains of the other modalities to compensate for the as yet undeveloped deductive capacities. This explains the mutual blockings and disturbances, which can be characterized as follows: on the one hand, the pseudonecessities attributed to all aspects of reality interfere, naturally, with the formation of possibilities; on the other, authentic necessity is based on systems of transformations and involves coordination between possibilities. It can, therefore, not be acquired in the absence of possibility. Pseudonecessities, of course, do not provide the reasons for a property or an event (this is particular to deductive necessity); still they show that subjects believe that these exist. However, they evaluate them as restrictive only, excluding all possible variation. Thus, reality is conceived of as too impoverished—with respect to possibility—but as overinclusive with respect to necessity. In this way, each of the modalities is altered as a function of the other two.

We can now understand why the development of operational structures is a consequence of another, more general evolution that cannot be explained in terms of operational development only. Operations require, in fact, a synthesis of possibility and necessity, the former characterizing their procedural freedom (flexibility), the latter their self-regulation and their system-bound compositions. If this is so, such constructions must have as preliminary conditions the formation of possibilities, the elaboration of necessities, and the progressive coordination of the two modalities. We reserve discussion of necessities to our second volume, but we can already see how the developmental levels we observed with respect to possibilities do in fact meet these conditions. Their convergence with the levels in operational development can be seen as an indication of a developmental process that goes from global to specialized forms. In no way can it be interpreted in terms of a primacy of operational structures. The fact that at level III the indeterminate and infinite co-possibilities come to merge with the hypothetico-deductive capacity of formal operations is thus only an indication that possibility and necessity have finally come to be differentiated and integrated with each other. It does not point to a leading role or primacy of operations; these, on the contrary, had to be constructed and elaborated.

But then, if possibility and necessity appear as the products of subjects' autonomous activity, what happens to reality once it is dominated and absorbed (in a manner of speaking) at both poles by capacities that are not derived from it? The latter restriction is, in a sense, too strong: the epistemic subject with her structures and, prior to this, the psychological subject with her problems and procedures are themselves part of reality, which includes the organism as a physico-chemical object and as the center of dynamic actions. If, then, in turn, the subject's actions and operations include reality in a network of possibilities and necessary relations, reality itself becomes correspondingly richer in that every real event appears as one actualization among others that are possible within a system of logico-mathematical transformations that provide explanations. There is a paradox of knowledge in that reality becomes more objective, its objects being analyzed more adequately, with an increase of deductive capacities. In other words, as possibility, reality, and necessity come to be differentiated, after an initial state of nondifferentiation, each of the three terms gets modified. This produces a new integration in which objects come to be incorporated in the subject with the help of mathematics and the subject becomes part of the object through biology: the operational structures issuing from this integration thus reveal their dual nature of necessary consequences and of instruments for new discoveries.

III

In several chapters, we have discussed the relations between the formation of possibilities and problems of equilibration. Our new observations not only extend our general model, which had seemed sufficient until now and which attempted to explain the operational structures by the mechanism of self-regulation, but also provide the key we were looking for to find a simple, direct answer to the most difficult question raised by our interpretations: By what mechanism do cognitive reequilibrations bring about, simultaneously and of necessity, compensations and novel productions—that is, an equilibration leading to advances (augmentative equilibration)?

Concerning the first point—that is, the simple generalization of the previous model—our comments in section II may suffice: by considering the operations not as the source but as a consequence of the formation of possibilities, once possibility, necessity, and reality are differentiated and coordinated, we subordinate possibilities and operational structures at the same time to the third type of our main forms of equilibration, that between differentiation and integration. At the initial level of nondifferentiation, there is disequilibrium and mutual interference between the three modalities, which explains why few possibilities appear initially. Their subsequent increase up to infinity results from this equilibration, and the development of operations results from the rebalanced coordinations between possibilities and necessities. Let us further recall that the equilibrium between differentiation and integration involves both compensations and constructions, since too much differentiation endangers the coherence of the whole and too much integration inhibits differentiation. In this case, as usual, equilibration amounts to mutual implication between intrinsic variations within a system that is both constructive and compensating.

But this is not the way that the consideration of possibilities revitalizes our equilibration model: rather it is by explaining the mechanism of reequilibration in terms of internal dynamics, specific to possibilities, in such a way that each new possibility constitutes simultaneously a construction and an opening because it generates, at the same time, a positive innovation and a new gap to be filled—a limitation and a disturbance to be compensated for. Put more simply, the birth of a possibility offers the dual aspect of a realizable conquest and the acquisition of a capacity that tends to be deployed, thus becoming the source of a new disequilibrium as long as it has not brought about a new conquest. In principle, one might say the same about any cognitive construction, from schemata to structures, and even about animal behavior, which is constantly driven by the two needs of extending the environment and increasing the organism's control of the environment. But even if this is quite general, one still has to make a distinction between the simple feeding of data into assimilatory schemata, which are only concerned with content, and the challenges (or problems) involved in accommodation, which give rise to procedures and modifications that appear possible or are rendered obligatory by the formal aspects of the process.

In fact, from the sensorimotor level on, one can distinguish four processes: (1) assimilations that function in the immediate present and lead to success; (2) accommodations that are similarly direct; (3) positive (obstacles) and negative disturbances (gaps and limitations), inhibiting (1) and (2) or opposing their realization; and (4) compensations that neutralize (3) and bring about new accommodations that become possible through a differentiation at (2) and that constitute, thus, the beginning of a procedure. This first initial phase in the production of possibilities, which can be observed in very young children, has not been studied in the preceding chapters. Still, we have called attention to two elementary processes that lead from one possibility realized to an opening up of the next. One has to do with the mechanism of choice: as soon as subjects understand an accommodation that is getting actualized as resulting from a choice, they realize that the solutions not selected become possibilities or at least point the way in which these can be constituted (see chapters 4 and 11). The other derives from the fact that any accommodation, once obtained in one context, can generate procedural transfers to analogous situations.

The dynamics of possibilities are more complex than these simple, directly observable openings of one possibility toward the next may lead one to suppose. There is also the fundamental fact that all of subjects' prior activities and experiences lead to the formation of new possibilities, not only to those that are immediately realized but also to what we might term *a field of virtualities*. Subjects who have solved certain problems, encountered disturbances, successfully carried out compensations—in short, differentiated, accommodated, and thus multiplied their assimilatory schemata by eliminating certain limitations—when confronted with situations that are entirely novel to them no longer find themselves in their initial state of "innocence." On the contrary, they are well aware that, since they were able to find a suitable heuristic in the past, this will enable them to find new ones for each novel situation. But in each new situation, the possibilities that may be constituted are not immediately available to the subjects. Therefore, the possibilities are not predetermined by what precedes them (as if one could speak of a change from potentiality to actuality). We do speak of a field of virtualities, but only in the sense that virtuality only represents the possibilities to be discovered (see chapter 6, where the level IA subjects, exploring the material, ask themselves whether—by acting in a certain manner—"it would be possible that [that] is possible," in the sense of physically realizable). There exists, thus, a more or less well-organized field that orients the subject in the direction of certain procedures that they already know, even though those to be discovered cannot be derived from the prior activities.

In a wide sense, each possibility thus produces a twofold result: a new actualization and a new deficit to be filled, an infinite sequence of reequilibrations. Unlike schemata and structures, which are simply sustained and generalized, being susceptible to enrichments, the procedural system introduces a specific type of dynamics based on a process that is simultaneously unbalancing and reequilibrating; this is the system of capacities acquired by the subject. Any generalization, while requiring the use of a procedure, is commanded or suggested by a new problem arising in the environment, the solution to which constitutes another adaptation to a new situation. In contrast, the specific nature of a capacity requires that it be exercised, commanding the production of variations that enable it to function; new possibilities are thus formed internally. We can distinguish two kinds of disturbances or limitations producing a compensation: the first come from the object (physical or logico-mathematical); these can be said to be real. The second consist in deficiencies within the subject, internal obstacles to the full use of the subject's own capacities (one may think of the uneasiness felt by an author who temporarily has no more ideas, or of that experienced by a child confronted with a material and the instruction to make "anything whatever" with it, when the child has no idea what to do with the material). The second type of disturbance is real if subjects are aware of it; it may be said to be virtual if subjects do not experience it consciously. But, in either case, disturbances function to drive transitions, which then turn out to be compensations despite their appearing to be spontaneous activities unrelated to equilibration. In short, possibilities, in general, as well as the field of virtualities, constitute a continuous source for reequilibrations, which are both constructive and compensatory. This is what we wished to demonstrate.

Possibility, inasmuch as it is related to capacity, constitutes simultaneously an instrument and the motor of reequilibration. Only two more essential facts remain to be mentioned. The first is that any possibility and procedural schema lead to presentative ones and, finally, to structures. The other is that structural generalizations start out as procedures. But these reciprocities do not pose any problem if one remembers that the "states" of equilibrium and disequilibrium characterize the presentative aspects of knowledge, whereas the specific role of the procedural aspect is to constitute the mechanism of reequilibration as such. In this way a relationship is established between the structuring, organizing activities of the epistemic subject and the needs and specific capacities of the psychological subject, which depend on the subject's history: structure as such does not, in fact, include "needs," yet it can present gaps. To be precise, one would also have to distinguish the individual capacities of a psychological subject from the variable strength or diversity of compositions in an epistemic structure. The fact that psychological subjects may have many traits in common can only induce us to replace the dichotomy of the psychological and epistemic by a trichotomy suggested by the work presently conducted by B. Inhelder: the individual, the common or general psychological (still temporal and causal), and the epistemic, which is nontemporal and exclusively implicational. In addition to its instrumental role in reequilibration, possibility thus ensures the transition from one level to the next (or between activity domains of the subject) in this particular hierarchy.

Index

Index

Accommodation, 95, 151: and choice, 90–91, 112; of constructions, 92
Actualization, 103, 105, 152
Algebra, commutative, 5
Analogy, 24, 26, 82, 109, 121: procedures of, 9, 22, 23, 37; successive, 10, 51–52, 92; and color, 11; and co-possibilities, 14, 82; transverse, 34–35; and operations, 36; boundaries, 50; modes of, 84; and pseudonecessity, 134; defined, 145
Aristotle, on motion, 5
Assimilation, 151
Asymmetry, internal, 146
Autonomy, 25

Berthoud, Ioanna, on metalanguages, 111
Bidimensionality, 82, 84, 85
Biggest, the, term, 83
Bipartitioning: of the square, 44–48; and duplication, 54; exhaustive, 57
Bolzano, Bernard, 5

Choices, discussed, 110–12
Cognitive systems, described, 5
Color, 8, 11, 12
Combinations, free, 61, 70
Compensations, 151
Completion, 121
Compositions: three-dimensional, 66; regulated, 81, 82, 84; free, 142; operational, 146. *See also* Overcomposition
Comprehension, and success, 107
Configurations, 8, 15

Consciousness, 110, 111
Constructions: and infinity, 17; tridimensional, 65; bidimensional, 85; and goals, 88, 90
Constructivism, 3, 4
Coordinate system, 18
Coordinations, 81, 122
Co-possibilities, 15, 22, 86, 96: in patterns, 10–11; abstract, 12–13, 14, 23, 24, 52, 59; concrete, 14, 23, 28, 97, 99, 145; deductive, 15; system of, 32, 36; and analogy, 51–52, 82, 84; formation of, 85, 106; anticipating, 103, 105; range of, 146. *See also* Possibilities
Deduction, 22, 23, 24, 78, 86, 107: and co-possibilities, 15; and variations, 17, 82; and possibilities, 37, 74, 77, 97, 99, 106; mechanism for, 147
Descartes, René, 18
Dichotomy, and axes of symmetry, 46
Differentiation: at level II, 35; trend toward, 109; lack of, 148; and integration, 151
Disequilibrium, failure as, 92–93
Distance, equal, 108, 112–13, 115, 118–19, 120–21
Disturbances, 151, 152
Division, 55, 56–57
Duplication: and bipartitions, 54; solving problem of, 57–58; comprehending, 59

Empiricism, arguments against, 3
Equilibration, 88, 93, 97, 152: forms of, 6,

151; mechanism of, 38, 146; progressive, 84; increasing, 88; factors in, 98
Extension, 135: unlimited, 60; of presentative schemes, 133
Extensive aspect, 22

Failure, as disequilibrium, 92–93
Fermat, Pierre de, and coordinate system, 18
"Forgetting" dimension, 24

Gaps, 98, 151
Generalization: at level II, 76; inductive, 107; defined, 122
Generation, modes of, 21–22
Geometry: Euclidean, 5; and space, 18
Goals: freedom and, 70; interpreting, 78, 81; unidimensional, 79, 81–82; and free constructions, 90; maintaining, 91; and errors, 93; and means, 121, 139, 145; defining, 122; presentative schema of, 143–44

Hamilton, Sir William Rowan, and algebra, 5
Hypotheses, formation of, 25

Improvement: behaviors aimed at, 85; following failure, 92; and reequilibration, 97
Inference, 77, 100, 103, 109: mechanism of, 22; deductive, 28, 104; retroactive, 57; operational, 106; extensional, 107; false, 118
Infinity, 24, 34
Inhelder, B., trichotomy suggested by, 153
Innovation, successive, 18
Integration, and differentiation, 151
Intension, 60, 135
Intensive aspect, 22

Kant, Immanuel, on geometry, 5

Largest possible, term, 78
Limitations: discussed, 11, 111–12, 134, 151; unintentional, 81; removing, 126; kinds of, 130, 152
Logic, internal, 14

Means: variability in, 78; and optimalization, 79; and goals, 121, 139, 145
Motion, Aristotle on, 5

Necessity: perception of, 15–16; and possibility, 78, 87, 149; and impossibility, 107; coordinations of, 122; as deductive mechanism, 147. See also Pseudonecessity
Negations, organization of, 38
Number, variations in, 76

Operations, 5, 16, 37, 38: and procedures, 24, 123; concrete, 33, 145; and analogies, 36; partitive, 49, 54; logical, 50; source of, 82; spatial, 83; and possibility, 87, 150
Optimalization: and means, 79; behaviors aimed at, 85; at level III, 98
Ordination, function of, 147
Overcomposition: and possibilities, 79, 84; defining, 81; initial, 82, 86. See also Compositions

Partitioning, 40, 43: and subtracting, 46, 48, 49; as procedural possibility, 49–50; exhaustive, 51; and symmetry, 52
Pathways, 23, 28
Possibilities: set of, 4; and analogy, 9, 11, 26, 37; abstract concepts of, 14; and necessity, 15, 78, 87, 147, 149; and sensorimotor skills, 18; spatial, 20; successive, 20–21; and deduction, 22, 37, 86, 97, 106; autonomous, 25; open system of, 32; partitioning and, 40, 49–50; number of, 47, 78, 106; reconstructions of, 57; and relativization, 59; instrumental, 62, 69, 74; physical, 70; and overcomposition, 79; and operations, 87; hypothetical, 92; and accommodations, 95; dynamics of, 96, 98; levels of, 99; and inference, 103; coordinations of, 122; relational, 140. See also Co-possibilities
Presentative schemes, defined, 4–5
Procedural schemes, defined, 5
Procedures, 24, 123: and analogies, 34–35
Pseudoimpossibilities, 5, 28, 136
Pseudonecessity, 5, 15, 25, 29, 32: and size, 81; notion of, 90; limitations and, 111, 112, 130; examples of, 129–30; and analogy, 134; of symmetry, 136. See also Necessity

Realizations, concrete, 57
Reciprocity, and possibilities, 96–97

Reequilibration, 88, 93, 97, 152. *See also* Equilibration
Relations: relations between, 82; initial, 84–85; perpendicular, 85; asymmetrical, 123; equivalence, 129
Relativization, and possibilities, 59
Rignano, Eugenio, on reasoning, 106
Russell, Bertrand, 4

Self-correction, 64
Self-regulation, determining, 6–7
Sensorimotor skills, 18, 36
Set of possibilities, term, 4
Shape, 12, 94: varying, 8; linear, 9, 10; regular versus "bad," 11; meanings of, 42
Size: variations in, 76; three dimensions of, 78, 85; interpreting, 80–81; and total surface, 81–82
Space, 18, 29
Subtraction, 54, 57: and partitioning, 46, 48, 49

Success: possibility of, 91; and comprehension, 107; and assimilation, 151
Symmetry: dichotomies and, 46; and co-possibilities, 52; internal, 129; and pseudo-necessity, 130, 136; and limitations, 134

Transfers: procedural, 21–22, 36; as categorial functors, 34; analogical, 37
Tripartitions, 48–49

Union, function of, 147

Value judgments, 8–9
Variations: intrinsic, 17, 76, 99, 123, 142; successive, 19; arbitrary, 22; initial, 84–85; co-possible, 96; extrinsic, 98, 123; quantitative, 147
Volume, 75

Weierstrass, Karl, 5
Weight, 75

Swiss-born psychologist **Jean Piaget** (1896–1980) taught at the Universities of Geneva and Lausanne. Among his many books published in English are *Language and Thought of the Child; The Moral Judgment of the Child; Play, Dreams, and Imitation; The Construction of Reality in the Child;* and *The Origins of Intelligence in Children.*

Translator **Helga Feider** earned a Ph.D. in linguistics at Indiana University in 1969, and is a professor in the department of psychology at the Université du Québec à Montréal.